PHONICS
THE EASY WAY

A clear and
comprehensive
guide to the
most up-to-date
methods for
**teaching your
child to read**

ANNIS GARFIELD

Illustrated by Alison Lingley

Vermilion
LONDON

Penguin Random House is committed to a sustainable future for our business, our readers and our planet.
This book is made from Forest Stewardship Council® certified paper.

5 7 9 10 8 6 4

Published in 2007 by Vermilion, an imprint of Ebury Publishing

A Random House Group Company

Text © Annis Garfield 2007
Illustrations by Alison Lingley 2007

The Random House Group Limited Reg. No. 954009

Addresses for companies within the Random House Group
can be found at www.randomhouse.co.uk

A CIP catalogue record for this book is available from the British Library

The Random House Group Limited makes every effort to ensure that the papers used in our books are made from trees that have been legally sourced from well-managed and credibly certified forests. Our paper procurement policy can be found on www.randomhouse.co.uk

Designed and set by seagulls.net

Printed and bound in Italy by Rotolito Lombarda S.p.A.

ISBN 9780091917173

Copies are available at special rates for bulk orders. Contact the sales development team on 020 7840 8487 or visit www.booksforpromotions.co.uk for more information.

The author and publisher have made all reasonable efforts to contact copyright holders for permission, and apologise for any omissions or errors in the form of credit given. Corrections may be made in future printings.

To buy books by your favourite authors and register for offers, visit www.penguin.co.uk

CONTENTS

Appendix: the Last Word

PREFACE

The word **phonics**, from the Greek, simply means **sounds**. **Synthetic phonics** describes the method of teaching a child to read using the **alphabetic code**, i.e. the child learns:

- the **sounds** of the letters of the alphabet
- to break the word down or **segment** it into its component parts, i.e. letter sounds
- to **blend** (synthesise) these letter sounds together again to read the whole word.

Thus the letter **a** is called **ay** and is sounded '**a**', as in **cat**; **b** is called **bee** and is sounded '**b**', as in **bat** and **c** is called **cee** and is sounded '**c**', as in **can**.

So the child, equipped with this alphabetic code, meets the word 'cab' and is able to break it down into its letter sounds (c-a-b), and then say the whole word 'cab'.

Phonics is not another experimental reading method. It has always been the traditional, problem-avoiding, universally successful method of teaching a child to read. This logical method has been tried and tested to work for all.

Phonics was largely ousted from schools from the 1950s onwards by a variety of laissez-faire, child-centred experiments such as Look and Say, Whole Books, Total Immersion and the like, where a child was invited to look at exciting words and guess or somehow learn them by heart by their overall shape or however he could. This, not surprisingly, has led to the steep decline in reading standards in our schools today. A hitherto unheard-of condition they call dyslexia was born – recognised neither by the BMA nor psychologists ('an emotional construct not a scientific function') – which is simply that miserable state of children who have not been taught to read. Surveys, reports and scientific evidence over the past ten years or so, and most recently a government review, have put this reading failure down to faulty

teaching methods and cite phonics as the solution. Curiously, if phonics has always been the rescue remedy for dyslexia, why was it not used first as a prevention?

The exclusive phonics teaching of reading is now, post-government review, compulsory in all our primary schools. The benefits of teaching the child the alphabetic code and showing him how, step by step, he can use it himself to reason out words so that he can really read will soon be apparent. This is the most important educational reform for decades; the irony being, of course, that it is not really a reform at all but simply a return – a modern, updated return – to proper standards and successful methods.

There are bound to be difficulties in the change-over period as teachers themselves adjust to the phonics system which may be unfamiliar to most. Given the importance of reading and the anomalies of our language it is obvious that as many parents as possible will want to teach their own children to read before they start school. DIY is best. In fact it would be an excellent idea for all children to be able to read before starting school, as in Russia.

The phonics programme in this book, following as it does the latest government recommendations, will be in line with current compulsory school teaching of reading.

Annis Garfield
2007

INTRODUCTION

The very greatest care must be taken in the teaching of reading. For, of all the skills we expect our children to learn, reading is not only the most important, but also potentially the most hazardous and very far from being 'as easy as ABC', an entirely misleading expression.

The child who learns to read confidently, fluently and well has a flying start in his whole education. The converse is also true: that early problems with reading can be difficult to overcome and leave a child with a lasting handicap in life. One of the greatest services a parent can do for a child is to ensure a trouble-free introduction to this essential skill; for confidence in reading will lead to confidence in everything else.

The phonic system of reading has recently been judged the most likely to succeed of all teaching methods, the best way to ensure that children read with fluency, accuracy, understanding and enjoyment. The excellent government programme to achieve decoding (reading) and encoding (writing), now compulsory in primary schools, is the basis of this book. This programme requires that the child must **be taught**: first to *sound* and *name* the letters of the alphabet; then to hear, identify, *segment* and *blend* phonemes (i.e. sounds) in words.

All the requirements outlined in the programme, including:

- identifying syllables in words, as in 'rob-in';
- sightreading of high frequency words such as 'does' and 'busy'(referred to in this book as Booby Trap Words);
- recognition of prefixes, suffixes and plurals (a-way, lift-ed, nose-s);
- appreciation of various spelling patterns, such as 'through' and 'tough'; and
- sound and letter patterns, rhyme and alliteration, such as 'naughty daughter', 'Scary Mary' and 'Freddie Frog';

are some of the essentials of the phonic system and have all been addressed in the following pages. It is significant that Professor Rose, the author of the government review and the new schools initial reading programme, goes out of his way to use the word 'taught'. This is a very welcome return to the recognition that children will not naturally pick up this essential skill of reading simply by being exposed to exciting books. It is sound and sensible to replace the Cloud Cuckoo Land notion that all children will automatically learn by some sort of osmosis, with one that involves formal **teaching** in a structured, graduated way.

Difficulties of the English Language

The hazards involved in learning to read the English language are notorious, with the inconsistencies of apparently simple words such as 'us' and 'is' (two different sounds of 's'); 'has' and 'was' (two different sounds of 'a'); 'arm' and 'warm'; 'comb' and 'bomb'. Not to mention obvious horrors such as 'cough', 'enough', 'through', 'though', 'bough', 'thorough' and 'bought', which seem designed to bewilder and confuse any child meeting them randomly and meeting them unprepared, unclassified and without explanation.

This book is, in short, a step-by-step logical arrangement of enough simple child-orientated English language to enable a child gradually to decode appropriate reading material. It is simply a sorting of the letter sounds in words. Children love to make order of things and, with help, can make sense of the complicated English language. With help from the graded, classified material this book provides, meeting no letter sound combination before it has been introduced, understood and learned, the child can be taught how to make sense of and work out for himself the initially baffling problems of words such as 'bead', 'bread' and 'steak', where the same spelling has different sounds; and, conversely, where the same sounds have different spellings as in 'cork', 'course', 'caught', 'nought', 'door' and 'warm'. These words are presented in due order, in the right category, at the right time, so that the child can understand that there is a system that works, and that he can use it himself. Even the oddest word has words similar to it. **Tongue** is not the one-off horror it can appear when grouped with its friends **guest**, **guide** and others. The child relishes being given a code, taught how to use it and finding that as a result of its correct application he can read. He is encouraged to use his reason, discouraged from guessing and finds that although a good visual memory does no harm, intelligent reasoning does better.

This phonic system, as Professor Rose has said, must be taught. The child must be taught the rules and how to apply them. He must be taught to decode a word, sound by sound, letter by letter, starting from the left and working to the right. He must not be tempted to guess. He must be taught how to encode (write) these letter sounds because reading and writing are a complementary process.

The Value of Nursery Rhymes and Talking

Nursery rhymes and other familiar rhymes are used a great deal in this book for the rhyme sound often helps the child to the sound of a difficult word:

Old King Cole
Was a merry old...

Hesitation over the unusual 'ou' spelling in **soul** will be readily overcome here because the child knows it must rhyme with **Cole**.

It cannot be stressed enough how important it is for children to talk, to be talked to from their earliest days and, most of all, to have stories read to them, and songs and rhymes sung with them and recited by them. Words, words, words should be with them as much as possible. This is the way the child will build up a valuable vocabulary of words in his head that will help more than anything with his reading. An articulate child, familiar with words, will learn to read more easily because the words are already there in his head. If confronted with the word **post**, for example, he might try the obvious short sound of 'o' first, the /o/ sound. There is after all **lost** and **cost**. But, with any luck, his own vocabulary will tell him that does not work so he will try the /o-e/ sound next, which does. The more words and word patterns you can instil into your child by reading and talking to him and encouraging him to speak, the better his reading and spelling will be.

Meanwhile the child must be taken through the phonic exercises. He must practise, practise, practise each step and each stage until he gradually gains confidence in his newly acquired skill. He must not be overwhelmed and thereby lose his confidence. He should not be asked to read words he is not ready for, or be faced with letter combinations he has not learnt. It may not be thrilling reading matter to begin with but he will be pleased to get his word sounds right and to be making progress. The more thrilling reading matter should be read *to* him until he can read it for himself.

HOW TO USE THIS BOOK

Throughout the book letters and their sounds will be referred to like this:

/a/ sound or /ee/ sound or /sh/

For example, the letter **a** is called **A/a** (as in cake), but, initially, makes the /a/ sound as in hat.

Not as in bath, which is the /ar/ sound;

Nor as in f**a**ll, which is the /**or**/ sound;

Nor as in **a**ny, which is the /**e**/ sound;

Nor as in w**a**s, which is the /**o**/ sound.

This will become clearer as the book is used. (The /**ee**/ sound means as in f**ee**t; and the /**sh**/ sound means as in **sh**ip.)

Children's Names

I've also included current children's names in each section. I have done so for various reasons:

- For fun: children enjoy seeing their name belonging to certain sound categories, or writing it in if it is not there.
- Familiar names are an excellent way of illustrating particular sound patterns. For example, **Ann**, **Ben** and **Tom** represent early, straightforward letter sounds; **James** and **Jane** show the effect 'e' has on vowels, turning /**a**/ into the /**a-e**/ sound; **Will-i-am** demonstrates how to break up a word into its constituent segments/syllables.
- In addition, names are more readily acceptable and memorable examples of the more difficult sounds the child will meet later in the book, for example **Grace** and **Christopher**.

Through names children are introduced early on to the idea that although, for example, 'g' to begin with has the hard /**g**/ sound, as in **get**, the name **George** has 'g' using the soft /**j**/ sound twice. **Francesca** is a good example of the /**ch**/ sound of c. **Lucy** and **Florence** are examples of the /**s**/ sound of c. **Lou-ise** illustrates several things: how 'ou' can have the long /**oo**/ sound; the importance of understanding segmenting and syllables; and how 'ise' can have the /**ee**/ sound – an apparently complicated lesson simply demonstrated in a popular name.

Names are also excellent examples of the necessity of sightreading of high frequency words. **George** and **Lucy** will have learned to recognise their names long before learning the phonic principle behind them: the /**j**/ sound of 'g', the /**or**/ sound, the /**oo**/ sound of 'u' and the /**s**/ sound of 'c', etc.

And finally, names are a very clear example of the unsounded letter principle: **Bill**, **Jack**, **Mick**, **John**, **Nell**, **Thomas**, **Anthony** and **Guy**. The stroke through the unsounded l, c, c, h, l, h, h and u respectively presents these words in a more user-friendly way.

Unsounded Letters

And now to address the unsounded letter:

duck quack knit when why lamb dumb through

For the learner reader who is struggling to give the right sound to all these new letters, the fewer letters and the simpler the word the better. So, the unsounded letter idea can be a great help to the beginner. For this reason, throughout this book unsounded, silent letters have been lightly crossed through with a line so the child can ignore it as he sounds the word out.

Initially the child will meet words ending with a double consonant, such as **ill**, **yell**, **buzz**, **whizz**, **odd**, **doll**, **cuff**, **stuff**, etc. As you work through the book, tell the child to ignore the second double letter when sounding out the word. Let him say **h-i-l** and then say **hill**. Let the child ignore the redundant letter. Of course, when he is writing them he must be reminded of their correct form.

Similarly, the 'ck' letter combination is very common in many simple, early words, such as **sick**, **back**, **tick**, **lock**, etc. A line through the unsounded 'c' presents the word in an easier form to the child.

Knee, **knot**, **knit**, **knife**, etc., can usefully have a line through their unsounded 'k' and **thumb**, **bomb**, **lamb**, **comb**, etc., will have one less problem for the tentative beginner reader if he is told to take no notice of the 'b'. **Whizz**, as seen above, can, of course, be doubly reduced with a line through the unsounded 'h' as well as through 'z'.

Prefixes and Suffixes

It is important for a child to recognise prefixes and suffixes, particularly for correct spelling. They show where a word may be broken up into the syllables essential for decoding it. Professor Rose has stressed the importance of prefixes and suffixes; that a child must recognise pattern in words. Take **beware** for example; it would be easy for a child not familiar with this word to get in difficulties by taking **bew** together and failing to get the word. If, however, he is aware of the prefix **be,** that it is a syllable, then he can tell where to break the word up and how to decode it.

Similarly with the word **away**; a child familiar with the phonics system, in general, and prefixes, in particular, will recognise the prefix **a** instead of getting nowhere trying **aw**. He will make a syllable of it and so the word will become both readable and spellable.

Therefore, throughout this book spaces have been put in to help the child recognise a word's component syllables. Many of these spaces are after prefixes and before suffixes and inflectional endings and plurals (such as **a** bout, patt **ed**, nos **es**, sing **ing,** every **where**). This recognition of prefixes, suffixes and word structure is fundamental to understand and to correct subsequent spelling.

And Finally ...

It would be a very good idea if every child learned to read at home before he started school. This has been the practice in Russia where children do not attend school until they are seven and know how to read. As for the **age at which to start reading** with your child, a question frequently asked, this varies enormously with each child and the family circumstances: the inclination of the child, the good or bad example of an older sibling, or the free time a parent or grandparent has available all have an impact.

Most children love the one-to-one attention of a parent or grown-up and at the age of three to sit on their lap and learn letter sounds. Some even read at three. Others do not formally want to learn their letters or anything else at four or even five. They should never be pressured or forced.

There are all sorts of games that can be played with letters and their sounds (I-Spy, alphabet counters, word games, painting, colouring, etc.). Until the child is five it should all be play, or very short learning-their-letters sessions and sounding out simple words. However, they can always be read to, talked to and encouraged to talk back, join in singing songs and reciting nursery rhymes – all of which will build up an increasing repertoire of words which will be an enormous help towards their reading when it comes.

Boys often are totally disinclined to sit still indoors with a clean, tidy book to read or write but will happily write their name on walls, dirty cars, steamed-up windows, etc. A girl, on the other hand, will enjoy sitting down to be industrious and competitive, to read her reading book and write neatly in her own writing book. A boy will often be more hesitant and unsure about sounding out and needs plenty of encouragement and praise. He likes to work words out logically and does not like to have to guess and be wrong.

A word of caution here: the greatest care must be taken that beginner readers are not hurried and overfaced. Ambitious parents should not expect too much too quickly from their children. Some children, as with all skills such as riding a bicycle and ball games, are more apt than others: their rate of progress varies along with their natural ability, willingness, confidence, commitment and determination. With something as crucial to his whole education as reading, the child must always receive unfailing patience, encouragement and confidence; for a problem created, allowed to develop and crystallise, will be hard to eradicate. Practise, practise, practise from graded classified material will work in time for all.

Above all, make it **fun**.

For ease and speed, and without wishing to offend the parents of girls, the masculine has been used for pronouns rather than alternating between male and female.

1

BACK TO BASICS – THE ALPHABET

THE BASIC ALPHABET
for learning the letters and their sounds

It is very important that the child knows the **sound** each letter makes. Initially, when the child is first learning his letters, the letters' sounds are more important than the letters' names. However, very soon it is necessary that the child knows both – i.e. that the letter **A/a** is called **ay** but sounds /a/ (as in bat) and so on. Therefore it seems sensible from the beginning to teach the child the sounds *and* the names of the letters; but it is the *sounds*, initially, that are more important.

Following are all the letters of the alphabet set out in their proper order. The current trend of introducing the child from the very beginning to a few letters at a time in order of popularity and out of their usual order (and calling it a fundamental of synthetic phonics) is unnecessary and can lead to subsequent confusion. Those letters and sounds that are the most common will, by their repetition and greater usage, necessarily become better established.

Watch out for the easily made confusion between the letters **b** and **d**. The illustration below often helps the child to distinguish between these two similar letters. Encourage the child to repeat **b-e-d** as he reads or writes.

Try to laugh when the inevitable mistakes with these two letters come and constantly remind the child of this tip for remembering which way round b and d go (or others: e.g. if his name includes one or other or both).

Another easily confused letter is **p**. The diagram below can help to establish **p**, especially if you tell the child the man is called **Peter**.

Peter

Teaching your Child the Alphabet

An important part of teaching your child to read and to write is to do it at his own pace so he is not put off and so that it remains fun and interesting for him. Some children will show more enthusiasm than others, so let your child make his own progress with learning the letters of the alphabet.

A rough guideline is to try and introduce two or three letters a day. On the first day, look at the letters A and B on page 21, sounding them together and then trying to write lower case 'a' and 'b' following the arrows on page 26. The next day, recap on A and B before introducing C and D in the same way. Some children will romp through their alphabet while others will need to build their confidence gradually by repetition and, of course, plenty of praise and encouragement. Ten minutes a day for a three- or four-year-old is ample.

Choose a time each day to sit down with your child and look at the letters together. It will be easier for both of you if these times are quiet, so avoid the background noise of television, radio or other distractions. If you have other children, choose a time when the baby is napping or the older children are at school. Avoiding times when your child is tired, hungry or thirsty can also make it easier for him to absorb the new information. Mornings are probably better than afternoons or evenings when your child is likely to be tired and finds it less easy to concentrate.

Children vary and so one child will relish the importance of a formal lesson sitting up at a table with the sole attention of a parent, while another will be made anxious by such ceremony and be overawed by the obvious high expectations of a pushy parent and therefore not do himself justice. For the latter child, casual references to letters or pointing at alphabet fridge magnets and talking about reading will be a positive introduction.

If you have a day when your child is simply not in the mood, avoid pushing the lesson for the day and start again tomorrow. He will learn faster and more effectively if he feels in control of the process and is motivated by your enthusiasm and plenty of praise.

As the letters are learnt you can reinforce the formal learning by pointing out the letters he knows when you find them in everyday places, such as on car number plates when you are out and about, on the cereal packet at breakfast time, on road signs, sides of buses, notices, etc. Have games with your child to find the letters his name begins with (sounding the letters, of course): 'Oh look, James! There's a 'j' for James.' Anything you can do to boost his confidence and enthusiasm for learning will benefit his reading skills. Try to enjoy it yourself and you will find your enthusiasm transfers to him!

Above all the child must not be overwhelmed. It should be fun not drudgery. Laugh if it is a bad day; read something entertaining to him and try again tomorrow. The child who wants to read whether he is three, four, five or older will then be keener to tackle the task of learning the alphabet and the letter sounds and stringing them together. The prospect of PlayStation games, all electronic games with letters and words, older brothers and sisters enjoying books, not to mention mobile phones, are all incentives and anything that inspires a child to read is good. If he sees you sitting down and reading a book or newspaper, let him know how much you enjoy reading and how interesting what you are reading is. Setting an example and making books part of everyday life will help as he begins to learn.

Patience and praise, praise and patience on the parent's part with constant repetition and practise of sounding out the words in the graded, classified order as set out in this book will achieve marvels.

A

ant

B

bed

C

cat

D

dog

E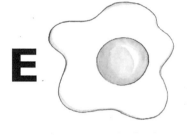

egg

F

frog

G

gate

H

hat

I

ink

J

jug

K king

L leg

M mug

N nose

O orange

P pig

Q queen

R rabbit

S 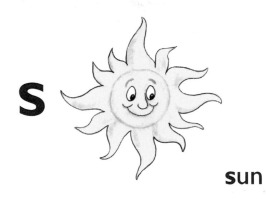 **s**un

T  **t**ap

U  **u**mbrella

V  **v**an

W 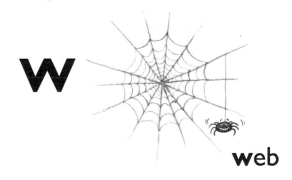 **w**eb

X  bo**x**

Y  **y**acht

Z  **z**ip

THE WRITING ALPHABET
to teach your child to write

The alphabet set out here is to teach the child how to form each letter: i.e. how to write each letter correctly. Make sure he holds the pencil correctly – between the thumb and the first two fingers. This is known as the 'tripod' grip (see below). Insist on the correct way even though it takes some time. An incorrect way quickly becomes habit and is difficult to change later. The parent will need to keep showing the correct way and constantly be ready to correct bad habits.

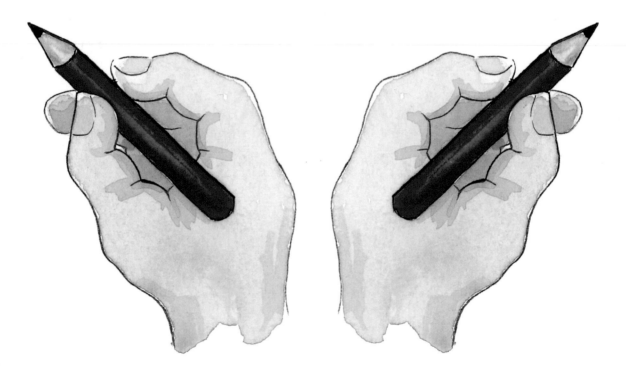

Bear in mind that reading skills and writing skills are acquired at different speeds. Girls are generally more skilled at writing at primary school age because they have better fine motor skills than boys and are largely more keen on drawing and writing. Don't worry about a child, especially a boy, being slow to get to grips with writing. There are no hard and fast rules here. Each child and situation is unique. Don't expect the letters to be known perfectly at once. Frequent repetition of the letter sound – **d** for example, saying the word **dog** in association with a dog picture – will gradually instil the letter in the child's mind. But expect confusion between this letter and **b**, as explained earlier (page 18).

Motivation is all. Some children will like to get to know and learn to write the letters of their own name or names of familiar things and this can be suggested to them. Some children will enjoy the achievement of doing so many letters a day, others will be more reluctant. Practise by going forward to new letters and then going back again. Throughout the book it is sensible to help the child do some new and some old every day. Let the child have his favourite letters or pages. It is also a good idea to move to new challenges before the old is perfectly known, then revising the previous exercises. Do not expect that the early pages will be learnt quickly. And remember that plenty of praise and encouragement is essential; even if progress seems very slow at first.

Writing the Alphabet

Show your child how to start at the dot and follow the arrow (see overleaf).

Below each letter there is a picture of something easily recognisable that begins with that letter in its primary sound, e.g. ant/bat. Give the following instruction to the child:

- *What can you see?*
- *Say the name.* Help the child to say ant.
- *Say the sound ant starts with.* Help the child to say **a-a-a**.
- *Now as you say a, write a starting at the dot and following the arrow.*

And so on through the alphabet. Let your child do the letters he likes first, lower case only in the beginning (capitals will come later – see page 33). Remember to refer back constantly. Let your child write his name whenever he likes.

Aa

say **a a a** as you write **a**

Bb

say **b b b** as you write **b**

Cc

say **c c c** as you write **c**

Dd

say **d d d** as you write **d**

Start at the dot and follow the arrows. Remember to say the letter **sounds** not names.
Tell the child the letter sound as he writes each letter.

Ee

say **e e e** as you write **e**

Ff

say **f f f** as you write **f**

Gg

say **g g g** as you write **g**

Hh

say **h h h** as you write **h**

Start at the dot and follow the arrows. Remember to say the letter **sounds** not names.
Tell the child the letter sound as he writes each letter.

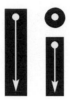

say **i i i** as you write **i**

say **j j j** as you write **j**

Kk

say **k k k** as you write **k**

Ll

say **l l l** as you write **l**

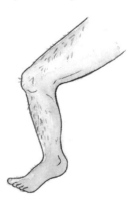

Start at the dot and follow the arrows. Remember to say the letter **sounds** not names.
Tell the child the letter sound as he writes each letter.

say **m m m** as you write **m**

say **n n n** as you write **n**

say **o o o** as you write **o**

say **p p p** as you write **p**

Start at the dot and follow the arrows. Remember to say the letter **sounds** not names.
Tell the child the letter sound as he writes each letter.

Qq

say **q q q** as you write **q**

Rr

say **r r r** as you write **r**

Ss

say **s s s** as you write **s**

Tt

say **t t t** as you write **t**

Start at the dot and follow the arrows. Remember to say the letter **sounds** not names.
Tell the child the letter sound as he writes each letter.

U u

say **u u u** as you write **u**

V v

say **v v v** as you write **v**

W w

say **w w w** as you write **w**

X x

say **x x x** as you write **x**

Start at the dot and follow the arrows. Remember to say the letter **sounds** not names. Tell the child the letter sound as he writes each letter.

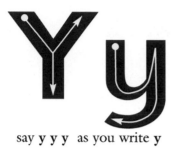

say **y y y** as you write **y**

say **z z z** as you write **z**

Start at the dot and follow the arrows. Remember to say the letter **sounds** not names.
Tell the child the letter sound as he writes each letter.

Capital Letters

Tell the child that his name, e.g. Ben, properly and correctly begins with a capital B. This need not be insisted on when first writing. Similarly, the child should be told that a sentence should begin with a capital letter and end with a full stop. This also need not be insisted upon until it is felt that the child has sufficient familiarity and acceptance of letters and words to understand.

Whether or not the child has got the hang of writing, you can and should proceed with the reading exercises in Section Two. Boys' writing particularly can be behind their reading – it is often untidy, uneven and misshapen. Praise, patience and perseverance nevertheless are paramount. Any device to achieve practise should be used by the parent of an unwilling or unmotivated child: writing a letter to Father Christmas, filling in blanks in sentences/notes/letters specially pre-written by the parent, writing on dirty car windows, etc.

A BRAVE NEW WORLD FOR YOUR CHILD – STARTING TO READ

SIMPLE THREE SOUND WORDS

Now that the child is beginning to recognise the letters of the alphabet and to know the sounds they make, **tell him that he can read**. This will boost his confidence. Now he can be helped to read his first simple words.

Tell the child to **start from the left** and from the **top of the page**. Keep repeating this: that to read English words you start from the left with the first letter sound, and move sound by sound to the right, to the end of the word. At this stage, when he is meeting individual words and simple sentences for the first time, this correct approach must be insisted on until it becomes habit. It is not obvious to a child and he must be told that a word or a group of words is not a picture to be looked at from any direction he likes but something to be decoded and he must start from the left.

Constant help and praise are all-important.

Point with a pencil or similar item to the relevant bit of the word. Cover part of the word if necessary to help concentrate the child's mind on the segment being read.

It is a good idea, throughout these reading exercises, for the parent and child to **take turns**. The parent/helper should read a bit and then the child. Constant repetition and revision are essential.

Particular care must be taken with bright, logical boys who quickly see the contradictions in our language and can often become confused and frustrated. 2+2 always equals 4 and 4x4 always equals 16. They may wonder why then 'get' is sounded **get**, but 'gem' is **gem**. Why is /**ea**/ different in 'bead', 'bread' and 'great'? Care must be taken to present these letter sounds in a graded classified order that the bright boy can reason out. Girls somehow are often more resilient, don't mind guessing and being wrong, and are not put off.

Segmenting and Blending

Help the child to sound out each letter and blend them together. Remind him not to over-emphasise the sound but barely to breathe it. This helps the blending of the letters into the word. Show him how the letter 'm' sounds as **mmm** rather than **muh**, which interrupts the fluency of the blending and makes reading more difficult.

So, for the word **mat** show the child how to sound out each letter separately: **m-a-t**. Then blend them together to say the whole word: **mat**. This is a simple three sound word.

Throughout the book letters and their sounds will be referred to like this:

- /a/ sound (in cat);
- /or/ sound (in cork, door, war, all, hawk, thought);
- /ee/ sound (in me, feet, meat, shield);
- /sh/ sound (in ship).

As mentioned above, the letter **Aa,** although called **ay** (as in cake) makes the /a/ sound as in hat.

- Not as in gate, which is referred to as the /a-e/ sound;
- Or as in bark, which is the /ar/ sound;
- Nor as in fall, which is the /or/ sound;
- Nor as in any, which is the /e/ sound;
- Nor as in was, which is the /o/ sound.

It is the **sound** that is important.

We have now reached the point of your child's first real reading. We are asking him to recognise letters, sound their individual letter sounds and blend them into a whole word. To make this easier, in the first exercise we are restricting the letters to eight: i.e. the vowel **a** and seven consonant letters. He has already seen the two alphabets at the beginning of the book in the normal alphabet order when practising sounds and writing.

BOOBY TRAP WORDS

These are words that do not fit into the general phonic rules. The child must learn these words by heart and will soon become familiar with them. You will find them highlighted in red throughout this section whenever they appear. (There will be different booby trap words highlighted in each section throughout the book.)

Only part of the word is irregular. Draw your child's attention to each word, as you come across it, looking carefully together at the part of the word that has to be learnt. With plenty of revision, he will soon get the hang of these booby trap words.

The booby trap words covered in this section are:

has   his   is   of   says   the   to

Aa /a/ sound as in 'van' – sound it out

Remember to tell the child that the letter is called **a** (as in c**a**ke) but makes the **/a/** sound (as in v**a**n).

Explain to the child that you are doing the **/a/** sound here with seven of the consonant letters that he has already met in the alphabet pages. Here we have taken the letters **a n t c r d g v**. Remind him of them again. Let him sound and write them again if he likes.

Now help the child blend these letter sounds into words. Help him sound out each letter separately and then blend them together into the whole word, i.e. say with him **c-a-t**, **cat**.

a   n   t   c   r   d   g   v

c-a-t   r-a-t   a-t

d-a-d   t-a-d

v-a-n   c-a-n   r-a-n

n-a-g   t-a-g   r-a-g

A   c-a-t   r-a-n   a-t   a   v-a-n

M-a-x   A-nn   D-a-n

F-a-n   J-a-ck   Ad-am

S-a-l   S-a-m   M-a-tt

Ee /e/ sound as in 'bed' – sound it out

Tell the child that **e** is called 'e' but sounds /e/ as in bed.

Explain to the child that you are doing the /e/ sound with four extra consonant letters. As before with /a/, remind him of them again and sound them out.

Say the sounds.

Help him to sound the letters out and blend them into the word.

Praise the child.

Repeat the /a/ sound.

e   b   l   p   m

B-e-n   p-e-n   m-e-n

m-e-t   p-e-t   l-e-t

p-e-g   b-e-g   l-e-g

b-e-ll   t-e-ll   b-e-d

T-e-n m-e-n m-e-t.

L-e-t B-e-n g-e-t a p-e-t.

N-e-ll, g-e-t a p-e-g.

Explain to the child that some letters are **unsounded** and will have a line through them until familiar. We have already met Jack and Matt and here we meet bell, tell and Nell.

B-e-n   J-e-n   L-e-n

T-e-d   N-e-d   E-d

N-e-ll

Ii /i/ **sound** as in 'pig' – **sound it out**

Five more letters; sound them out again.

i   l   k   w   x

Help the child sound out these words.

(p-i-n)   b-i-n   w-i-n

Say the letter sounds.

k-i-t   b-i-t   s-i-t

s-i-x   m-i-x

Say the sounds.

p-i-g   b-i-g

Repeat the pages again. Go back to the beginning.

p-i-ck   s-i-ck

Explain to the child how **is** and **as** are sounded.

A   b-i-g   p-i-g   i-s   s-i-ck.

J-i-m   i-s   i-ll.

Let the child do some old and some new pages every day. Let him repeat lessons until fluent and have a favourite page. Accept that some days are bad days: laugh and try again tomorrow. Try to avoid your child becoming overwhelmed, frustrated or bored. Don't forget to make a fuss of him and how clever he is now that **he can read**.

G-i-ve   h-i-m   a   p-i-ll.

K-i-t   i-s   a   k-i-d.

B-i-g   a-s   a   p-i-g.

F-i-nn   B-i-ll   K-i-t   B-i-d

W-i-ll   Ph-i-l   J-i-ll

Ii /i/ sound

Oo /o/ **sound** as in 'dog' – sound it out

Sound out these letters and then these words.

Say the sounds.

o   s   h   f
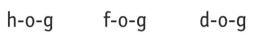

h-o-g   f-o-g   d-o-g

h-o-t   p-o-t   r-o-t
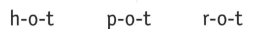

s-o-ck   c-o-ck

f-o-b   s-o-b   t-o-p

Tell the child how **of** and **to** are sounded.

A d-o-g g-o-t o-n t-o-p
   o-f a l-o-g.

N-o-d, T-o-m, n-o-d to J-o-hn.

Repeat the pages again.

A c-o-ck g-o-t o-n a r-o-ck.

J-o-hn   T-o-m

J-o-ss   R-o-b

Oo /o/ sound

Uu /u/ sound as in 'mud' – sound it out

Help sound out five more letters.

Help the child sound out the words.

u w j y z

b-u-g   j-u-g

h-u-t   b-u-t

w-e-t   y-e-t

s-u-n   r-u-n

b-u-zz   f-u-zz

S-i-x m-e-n d-u-g a p-i-t.

B-u-g i-n a r-u-g.

F-u-n i-n a h-u-t.

MIXED SENTENCES

Explain to the child how **the** is sounded.

Dot Dog has a den in the sun.
Dot Dog has a run in the mud.

Remind the child how **has** and **of** are sounded.

Dot Dog has a dig in the mud.
A lot of mud, a lot of muck,
  a lot of mess.

Let us get on the bus.
Let us sit at the top.

Take it in turns to read with the child.

G-u-s   R-u-ss   D-ou-g

Explain to the child how **the**, **says**, **has** and **his** are sounded.

Tell the child that **have** has an unsounded 'e'.

Explain to the child that when they see the speech mark (') it indicates that someone in the story is talking. And that when the person is finished talking they will see another mark ('). You can help the child understand this if, when it's your turn to read, you do a different voice for the characters when they speak. Encourage your child to recognise speech marks and try a funny voice.

FUSS on a BUS

Can Pip Pig get on a bus? Yes, but Miss Pat-Pat, the cat, will fuss. Miss Pat-Pat will fuss if a pig is on the bus.

'I will not get on Miss Pat-Pat's lap,' says Pip Pig, 'I will not kiss her. Yuk! But I have to get to the vet. I have a bad leg.'

And Pip Pig has a big red sock on his bad leg.

mixed sentences

Tell the child that 'of' is sounded **of**, but 'off' is **off**; 'is' is **is**, but 'miss' is **miss**; 'us' is **us**, but 'fuss' is **fuss**.

45

'I will not have a pig on the bus. I am a top cat. I will not have it.

'Bill!' (Bill is the boss man on the bus. Bill has a red cap.)

'Bill, toss him off the bus. Get off, Pig. Oh, oh, oh. Muck on the bus. Meg Hen, mop up the mess.'

But Meg Hen will not mop up the mess.

'I will not,' says Meg Hen. 'Miss Pat-Pat is a bad cat. Pip Pig is not bad.'

mixed sentences

Six big men met Miss Pat-Pat. Six men in a van met the bus. The men will fix the fuss. The men led Miss Pat-Pat off to the red van. Miss Pat-Pat can sit in the van and get to the hut on the hill. 'I live in a hut on the hill,' says Miss Pat-Pat.

Pip Pig can get on the bus. Pip Pig and his bad leg can get to the vet.

Go back to the beginning of the book and start again so the child becomes familiar with the lessons that have come already.

mixed sentences

FINAL 'S'

Here we meet the **final s** (as in plurals, and wherever they come, as in si**t**s and rap**s**).

Tell the child first to sound out the letters, e.g. b-a-g, then blend them into **bag** then sound out **s** and blend the whole word into ba**gs**.

Remind the child of the **/v/** sound in **of**.

Praise the child and remember to repeat earlier pages.

Do some new exercises and some old ones every day. This will reinforce everything your child has learnt so far and help his confidence to grow.

dog-s on log-s   leg-s on peg-s

bug-s in rug-s   lot-s of dot-s

bit-s and bob-s   cat-s and dog-s

mum-s and dad-s   can-s of fizz

pick-s up pin-s   lock-s the box

lot-s of hug-s   rat-s in den-s

GETTING DOWN TO BUS-I-NESS – VOWELS AND CONSONANTS

SOME LONG VOWEL SOUNDS
/a-e/ /ee/ /i-e/ /o-e/ /u-e/

Here we briefly meet some long vowel sounds which we will see more of later:

/a-e/   /ee/   /i-e/   /o-e/   /u-e/

Tell the child to sound the words out as usual: r-**ay** using the long sound of each of these vowels. Later, of course, the child will learn that the letter combination **ay** makes the /a-e/ sound; that the letter combination **ea**, as in t**ea**, and **ey**, as in k**ey**, can make the /ee/ sound. But here **unsounded** letters are referred to.

BOOBY TRAP WORDS

Remember from Section Two that Booby Trap Words are words that do not fit into the general phonic rules. Therefore your child needs to learn these words by rote. You will find these words highlighted in red throughout this section whenever they appear.

/a-e/ sound, as in gate	r**ay**	p**ay**	w**ay**	m**ay**	
	d**ay**	s**ay**	j**ay**	b**ay**	
/ee/ sound, as in feet	h**e**	k**ey**	m**e**	b**ee**	
	t**ea**	w**e**	f**ee**	s**ee**	
/i-e/ sound, as in bite	d**ie**	h**igh**	l**ie**	m**y**	
	s**igh**	t**ie**	**I**	p**ie**	
/o-e/ sound, as in bone	b**ow**	g**o**	J**o**	J**oe**	
	kn**ow**	l**ow**	m**ow**	n**o**	s**o**
/u-e/ sound, as in blue	S**ue**	bl**ue**	d**o**	y**ou**	
	tw**o**	t**oo**	t**o**	wh**o**	
	b**y**	m**y**	b**uy**		

BOOBY TRAP WORDS

Tell the child that **who** is sounded like **do** or **coo**; and that unlike most of the other **wh** words, the w is not sounded.

yell

yes

yet

Explain to the child that the letter **y** can also have the /i-e/ sound as in b**y**. Tell the child the difference between y as a consonant and y as a vowel.

some long vowel sounds

Pat has **no** hat.

Bill has **no** mill.

Nell gets two bells.

Di gets **no** pie.

I s**ee** a b**ee** in my te**a**-cup.

Is it on m**y** lip?

No, it will d**ie** in m**y** te**a**.

S**ue** m**ay** b**uy** a bun.

J**oe** m**ay** b**uy** a mug.

Will m**ay** b**uy** a jug.

I will give you a big hug.

Dad will give me a big hug.

My dog gives me a wet lick on

my leg.

We will kiss Mum.

Jo   Joe   Guy

Sue   Di   Fee

some long vowel sounds

SIMPLE TWO SYLLABLE WORDS

Explain to the child about syllables: a syllable is the unit of spoken sound; a syllable is like a beat in a word, e.g. **Sam** has one syllable or beat, **Me-gan** has two syllables or beats and **Dom-in-ic** has three. This will help in segmenting a word.

Do some new pages and some old every day.

Tell the child to spell/sound out the word in two bits or syllables and then put them together.

w-i-g   wig

w-a-m   wam

wig wam

Don't try to tackle all these words at once. Choose some lines one day and some another day.

Praise the child.

Tell the child that these vowels are long sounds and help him with a pencil mark over the long vowel sound i.e. bāy, pīe.

sun set	lap top	bin bag
pic nic	cob web	hot pot
sea sick	pock et	pack et
jack et	cock pit	tick et
wick et	wick ed	pig let
rob in	rab bit	hor rid
lem on	but ton	les son
list en	bot tom	kit ten
bit ten	sud den	
can not	par rot	car rot
cam el	pan el	ken nel
tun nel	pet rol	
la bel	ba con	e vil
i pod	pi lot	li on
si ren	o pen	e ven
tu lip	ha zel	
yel low	fel low	fol low
hol low	pil low	wil low
win dow	el bow	

simple two syllable words

The pi lot will sit
In the high cock pit
Of his jum bo jet,
And go to Tib et.

In the pock et of my jack et
Is a tick et for the bus.
If you get a tick et, Jan et,
You can sit with us.

My kit ten
Has bit ten
My mit ten
To bits.

Tell the child how **for** and **with** are sounded. They will be covered later.

Rob in	Thom as	Is o bel
Col in	Har ri et	Ad am
Hel en	Al ec	Da vid
Si mon	Yas min	Dan i el
Meg an	Pat rick	Wil li am
Mo ham med	Cos mos	Dom in ic
Ev an	Ben ja min	Ru fus

simple two syllable words

TWO SYLLABLE WORDS WITH FINAL 'Y'

Remind the child of **y** sounding:

/**y**/ as in **y**es

/**i-e**/ as in b**y**

Now tell him **y** can sound /**i**/ at the end of a word as in sil**ly**.

Explain that **many** has the /**e**/ sound.

Tell the child that **u** here sounds like **i**.

BOOBY TRAP WORDS

Busy: This is a funny word but think of Busy Lizzie and you'll be all right.

/a/ sound

Dad dy	hap py	car ry
mar ry	mad ly	bad ly

/e/ sound

pen ny	man y	mes sy
mer ry	ver y	jel ly

/i/ sound

sil ly	kit ty	diz zy
bus y		

/o/ sound

bod y	hol ly	jol ly
pop py	lor ry	sor ry

/u/ sound

pup p**y**	lu̸ck **y**	ug l**y**
bun n**y**	fun n**y**	sun n**y**
hur r**y**	fuz z**y**	

long vowel sound

ba b**y**	la d**y**	dai s**y**
la z**y**	ea s**y**	ti d**y**
ti n**y**	ho l**y**	po n**y**

Tell the child these are long vowel sounds.

Explain that **I'm** is short for **I am** and that /'/ shows that a letter is left out.

Isn't is short for **is not**.

Didn't is short for **did not**.

Take it in turns.

Bil ly, I'm sor ry
You fell off the lor ry,
But isn't it lu̸ck y
You didn't get mu̸ck y?

It is ea sy
To be la zy
On a ha zy sun ny day.

My old man
Said, 'Fol low the van,
And don't dil ly dal ly on the way.'

BOOBY TRAP WORDS

Explain how **said** is sounded and that **don't** is short for **do not**.

Old is another special word to be learned by heart.

two syllable words with final 'y'

Remind the child about capital letters: that they come at the beginning of sentences and the start of names.

Tell the child that **ie** at the end of a word can sound the same as **y**. So that Lizzy can also be Lizz**ie**, and Fredd**y** can be Fredd**ie**.

Ric̷k y	Pen ny	Em mie
Ed die	Pop py	A my
Ka ty	Mol ly	John ny
El lie	Tom my	Sal ly
Jac̷k y	An nie	Har ry
Kit ty	Lil y	Bil ly
Ro sie	Zo e	Mil lie
Min nie	Es me	Al fie
Al i	Hen ry	Hol ly
Mal ly	Mad dy	Ol lie
Pam my	Zo e	To by

CONSONANT COMBINATIONS

Now we meet two and (sometimes three) consonants together:
at the beginning of the word – as in **St**-an;
at the end of the word – as in sa-**nd**;
at both the beginning and end of the word – as in **st**-a-**nd**.

Help the child to blend the two consonants together as one and sound out the word as usual:

St a n   **St**an

s a **nd**   sa**nd**

st a **nd**   **st**a**nd**

Help him to identify the sounds and blend them together by patience and practise, repetition and encouragement. Don't let him guess but encourage him to reason it out. Point with a pencil to the first sound, breathe out the sound for him if necessary and block out the rest of the word.

Tell the child that s and t are sounded together **st**. Let him sound out **nest**.

n e **st**   ne**st**

Don't try to tackle all these words at once. Choose some lines one day and some another day.

ne **st**	be **st**	te **st**
pe **st**	gu̸e **st**	fi **st**
twi **st**	du **st**	lo **st**
mi **st**	cru **st** y	

st u b	**st** i ¢k	**st** u f̸f
st i ll	**st** a g	**st** ay

st op

Similarly, help the child to sound out these three sound words.

h a **nd**	b a **nd**	s a **nd**
st a **nd**	m e **nd**	b e **nd**
le **nd**		

consonant combinations

se **nd**   se **nse**   nonse **nse**

fr/e **nd**   po **nd**   fo **nd**

sk ip   **sk** in   de **sk**

hu **sk**   bri **sk**

sl u g   **sl** a p   **sl** a m

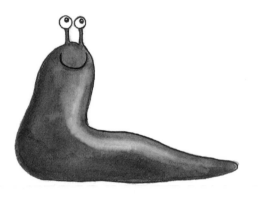

sn u g   **sn** i ff   **sn** i p

sn a ¢k   **sn** o w/

Sn ug as a bug in a rug.

Remember to take turns
reading with the child if he likes,
and constantly praise him.

Remind the child how **the** and **says** are sounded and that they will be explained later.

FRED DY FROG AND BLACK RAT HAVE A PIC NIC

Chapter One

Fred dy **Fr**og sits on his lil y pad. He sits on his lil y pad in the po **nd** in the sun a **nd** kicks up his legs.

'Hum, hum,' says **Fr**ed dy **Fr**og. 'I am **gl** ad to see it is a sun ny day. **Ple n t y** of **fl** ies to day.

Bl ack Rat sits in the du **st**. He sits ver y **st** ill in the du **st** on the ba **nk** of the po **nd**. He is sad. He is sad and un hap py. '**Sn** iff, **sn** iff,' he goes sad ly.

'Le**nd** a **fr**ie**nd** a pot of **sl**ugs, **Fr**ed dy,' says **Bl**ack Rat. I mu**st** have a **sn**ack. I had bad luck to day. I lo**st** my **sl**ugs when I fell off my log. I had the pot in my pocket and I mu**st** have lo**st** the lot. I have not got a **sl**ug. I have not got a **sn**iff of a **sl**ug. No tea for me un less you can le**nd** a ha**nd**. I am very fo**nd** of **sl**ug hot pot.'

(Continued on page 66.)

consonant combinations

MORE CONSONANT COMBINATIONS

sp e ll	**sp** i ll	**sp** i **lt**
st a **mp**	c a **mp**	l a **mp**
l u **mp**	b u **mp**	

gr i n	**gr** u nt	**gr** o w

cr a b	**cr** u mb	**cr** o ss
a **cr** o ss	**cr** ay on	

fr o g	**fr** ee	**fr** y

br i ck	**tr** i ck	**tr** u ck
tr a p	**tr** ee	**tr** ue

dr u m	**dr** o p	**dr** y

pr a m   **pr** e ss   **pr** ay

pr o b lem   **pr** o m ise   **pr** e te nd

fl a g   **fl** o ck   **fl** y

pl u m   **pl** e nt y   **pl** ay

gl a d   **gl** ue   **gl** ow

bl o t   **bl** a ck   **bl** ow

bl ue

cl o ck   **cl** a p   **cl** i ff

scr a p   **scr** u b   **spr** ay

str ay   **str** i p   **str** a p

tw e lve   **tw** in   **tw** i g

m i **lk**   s i **lk**   fi **lm**

FRED DY FROG AND BLA CK RAT HAVE A PIC NIC

Chapter Two

'Well, well,' says **Fr**ed dy **Fr**og. 'I am sor ry for you, **Bl** a ck Rat. But why not **sc**r ap the **sl** ug hot pot? Wh y not **sw** im a **cr** oss the po **nd** and have a pic nic on my lil y pad? Can you see my ca **mp** and my **fl** ag? It will be fun. I have **pl** en ty of **gr** ubs and big fat **fl** ie s. My **gr** ub **fr**y up is the be **st**, I **pr** om ise you. A **nd** I can **gr** ill **fl** ies in **cr**umb s and mix mugs of fiz zy **st** uff.'

Fred dy **Fr**og li ck s his lips. 'I will be **gl** ad to have you. No **pr** ob lem. **Gr** u **nt**, **gr** u **nt**,' goes **Fr**ed dy **Fr**og.

So **Bla**ck Rat **cl**aps his ha**nd**s, and says, 'Yip pee.' He **cl**aps his ha**nd**s and **gr**ins. 'I am on my way, **Fr**ed dy.' And he ju**mp**s in to the po**nd.**

He **sw**ims lick et y **spl**it acr oss to the big ge**st**, be **st** lil y pad. And on the big ge**st** be **st** lil y pad is the big ge**st** be **st** pic nic a **fr**og can do. 'Yum yum,' says **Bl**ack Rat hap pi ly.

Explain that in many words beginning **wh,** the **h** is unsounded:

wh en   wh y

Clar iss a   Cres si da   Mat ild a

Ind i a   Wil frid   Seb ast i an

Ron ald   Greg or y   Fred die

Fred e rick   Sask i a   Ed mund

Ben e dict   Benj a min   Ga bri el

Clem ent ine Pat rick   Ste phen

more consonant combinations

/AR/ /ER/ /OR/ SOUNDS

The letter **r** does funny things to vowels, i.e. to /a/, /e/, /i/, /o/ and /u/ which we'll deal with properly later on. But let's quickly meet:

/ar/ sound	c**ar**	f**ar**	j**ar**	
/er/ sound	f**ir**	s**ir**	h**er**	f**ur**
/or/ sound.	**or**	f**or**	be f**ore**	s**ore**

Sound the words out again in syllables.

	l e t	**let**
Then:	–t er	
Then:	**let ter**	

let t**er**	bet t**er**	but t**er**
gut t**er**	lit t**er**	sit t**er**
ot t**er**	pot t**er**	en t**er**
sis t**er**	Mis t**er** (Mr)	win t**er**
din n**er**	sum m**er**	sup p**er**

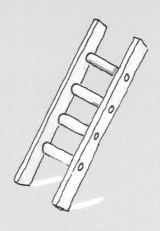

Remind the child that these vowel sounds are long and help him with a pencil mark over the vowel sound i.e. bōw, Sūe.

nev **er**	ev **er**	riv **er**
lad d**er**	rob b**er**	rub b**er**
un d**er**	su p**er**	cor n**er**
mar ket	**gar** den	**tar** get
ma k**er**	ba k**er**	Pe t**er**
pi p**er**	di v**er**	o v**er**
mo **tor**	mo **tor** way	so **fa**
mo **tor** car	doc **tor**	ac **tor**
yes **ter** day		

Rab bits
Have sil ly hab its.
They sit in the way
Of mo **tor** ca**r**s and say,
'Su per day
We won't go a way.'
Do zy!
Mes sy!

BOOBY TRAP WORDS

They and **won't** are difficult words your child will have to learn.

/ a r / / e r / / o r / s o u n d s

Nev **er**, ev **er**

Go un d**er** a lad d**er**

Or you will have bad luck.

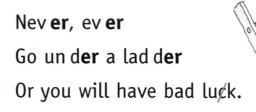

Take it in turns reading.

Nev **er**, ev **er**

Go o v**er** a riv **er**

Un less you can go as a duck.

Leg o v**er**,

Leg o v**er**

The dog ran to Do v**er**.

And at the big riv **er**,

Hop, he got o v**er**.

Osc ar   Hec tor   Dex ter

Am ber   Al ex an der

Pe ter   Hon or   Han nah

El ean or   Ol i ver

Let the child go back to the start of Section Three and do some old pages and some new. Try to do two old pages and one new each time.

/ ar / / er / / or / sounds

S AND H: sh sh sh

Tell the child that **s** and **h** can be sounded together to say **sh**.
Say **sh sh sh**.

Sound out the words as usual.

Don't try to tackle all these words at once. Choose some lines one day and some another day.

Explain how **ch** is sounded **sh**.

sh o p	**sh** e ll	**sh** i p
sh el ter	**sh** e d	**sh** o ck
sh aggy	**sh** ad ow	**sh** all ow
sh ut up		
di **sh**	di **sh** es	wi **sh**
fi **sh**	wi **sh** es	ma **sh**
ca **sh**	cr a **sh**	da **sh**
ha **sh**	fl a **sh**	spl a **sh**
hu **sh**	ru **sh**	bru **sh**
rad i**sh**	van i**sh**	pol i**sh**
pun i**sh**	rub bi**sh**	
Brit i**sh**	Scot ti**sh**	Wel **sh**
I ri**sh**	En gli**sh**	
Sa ch a	Ch ar lotte	

TRI SH FI SH VAN ISH ES

Tri **sh** Fi **sh**, in a ru **sh**, **sh** ot up the riv er.

'I am sor ry I can not stop, Min nie,' she said to her friend, Min nie Min now.

'I am in a hur ry. **Sh**... **sh**... hu **sh**, hu **sh**,' she whisp ers. 'Ol lie Ott er must not see me. Hor rid Ol lie Ot ter wants fi sh on a di **sh** for his din ner; not any fi **sh**, he says; he wants me, Tri **sh** Fi **sh**.

'But he will not get me on a di **sh** for his din ner. Not if I can help it. Ol lie Ott er can have any fi**sh** but me. So I am off as quick as I can. I must

Tell the child how **qu** sounds.

s and h

hop, skip and jump across to the **sh**allow bit of the river. I must van**ish** so he cannot see me. I must van i**sh** behind the big rock.'

And off **sh**e goes in a hurry. **Sh**e goes behind the big rock in the **sh**allow bit of the river. Nobody can see her. It is not easy to see Tri**sh** Fi**sh** in the **sh**adow.

Ollie Otter swims up the river.

'Hello, Minnie Minnow,' he says to Minnie as he goes by. 'Did Tri**sh** Fi**sh** go by?'

'Oh, no, Ollie Otter,' says Minnie, and **sh**e crosses her fins as **sh**e tells a tiny lie for

her friend. Min nie blu sh es as
sh e tells him, 'No, Tri **sh** Fi **sh**
is up the riv er to day. Umm…
er… **Sh** e went far, far a way
to see her sis ter.'

Ha mish   Char lotte

Nat ash a   Sash a

CH TCH

Explain to the child that the letters **c** and **h** together make the sound **ch** (as in **ch**a **ch**a **ch**a) and you will find it at the beginning of a word, **ch**in, and at the end, mu**ch**. You will also find **tch** at the end of words as in i**tch**.

ch a t	**ch** i ck en	
ch i p	**ch** i n	**ch** o p
ch op stick	**ch** oc o late	**ch** im ney
ch ild ren	**ch** ub by	**ch** u m

c a **tch**	m a **tch**	scr a **tch**
w i **tch**	f e **tch**	str e **tch**
cr u **tch**	h u **tch**	i **tch**
k i **tch** en		

m ar **ch**	ar **ch**	b en **ch**
r i **ch**	t ou **ch**	wh i **ch**
in **ch**	p in **ch**	m u **ch**
s u **ch**	s and wi **ch**	

BOOBY TRAP WORDS

Explain the /a-e/ sound in neighbours here even though we have not yet covered it. This is another word which must be learned by heart and practised.

Tell the child that **an** means the same as **a**. It is put before words beginning with the letters a, e, i, o and u because otherwise they are difficult to say.

Try saying **a ant**. Difficult?

Then say **an ant**. Easy!

Tell the child how **one** and **two** sound.

Which and **what** are two more words where the unsounded letter will help your child to learn them.

Cross pa **tch**
Shut the la **tch**
Sit by the fire and spin.
Get a cup
And drink it up,
Then call your neigh bours in.

If I have an i **tch** on my leg
I simp ly have to scr a **tch** it.
But it isn't much fun
If I can not rea **ch** or t ou **ch** it.

I know two twins,
Ri **ch** ard and Mi **tch**;
But I nev er can tell
Whi **ch** one is whi **ch**.

Rich ard   Ra chel

ch tch

76

THIS, THAT AND THE OTHER

t and **h** are sounded together:

Explain to the child that **t** and **h** together sound **th** as in **th**is, **th**at and **the** other. We have already met **the**. There are lots of other words like **the**.

BOOBY TRAP WORDS

Tell the child that **o** is sounded **u** in:

bro th er
come
done
Lon don
mo th er
o th er
o ven
some

Help him learn these words.

th th th

the	**th** en	**th** is
th at	**th** an	**th** em

wi **th**	w ea **th** er	b o **th** er
sl i **th** er	ei **th** er	n ei **th** er
m a **th**s	b o **th**	

th in	**th** ink	**th** i ck
th umb	**th** row	**th** ree
th rough		

tr u **th**	t ee **th**	cl o **th**
m o **th**	fr o **th**	

If the wea **th** er is hot,
Th en I swim a lot.
If it's not hot wea **th** er,
Th en I don't much bo **th** er.

Explain how **a** is sounded like **o**.

BOOBY TRAP WORDS

Here we need to look at **does**.
Music gives me a buzz;
It really does.

The nor**th** wind does blow,
And we shall have snow,
And w**h**at will **th**e rob in do
th en, poor **th** ing?

Tom **Th** umb
Lives on cr umbs.
Th ick as my **th**umb
Th in as a pin.

Cried **Liz zie**,
'I'm **bus y**,
I'm b**u**ild ing a house.'

'No **hur ry**.
Don't **wor ry**,'
Said lit tle Miss Mouse.

This rhyme also helps with the
/**u**/ sound in **worry**, which is a
bit odd until you think of all the
other **o** spellings which have the
/**u**/ sound.

I sho ved my cou sins in the o ven.
My br oth er said,
'Oh! Don't you love them?'
'Not m uch,' I said. 'I'll tell you st uff
Ab out them, that they're very r ou gh
On Kit ten-Cat. And very t ou gh.'

WH WORDS
Where **h** is unsounded like:

which   when   why

where   what

Also:

whiz   whack   wheel

whip   whis per   whole

But beware of another booby trap
in **who** where **w** is unsounded.

Who or why or **which** or **what**,
Is the A kond of Swat?
Does he wear a tur ban,
    a fez or a hat?
Does he sleep on a matt ress,
    a bed or a mat,
Or a cot, the A kond of Swat?

What takes us into the /o/ sound of **a**, as in:

wh**a**t	w**a**sh	squ**a**sh
w**a**sp	w**a**s	w**a**nt
w**a**nd	w**a**l low	sw**a**l low
w**a**tch	w**a**sh ing	m**a**ch ine

OZ ZY WOZ ZY

Oz zy Woz zy w**a**s a wasp.
She longed to be a trac tor.
'That's not a job for wasps,' said Dad.
Her moth er went and wh**a**cked her.

'Wh**y** shouldn't I be wh**a**t I want?'
Said Oz zy ver y sad ly.
'Just w**a**tch me be a trac tor wasp.
I'd do it ver y glad ly.'

Ra chel	Rich ard	Fran cesc a
Ch arlie	Tab i tha	Ruth
Na than	Jon a than	Cath er ine
Beth	E liz a beth	Theo

NG NK ENDINGS

Here are two more useful consonant combinations like **sh**, **ch** and **th** that are sounded together. **ng** and **nk** often come at the end of a word, never at the beginning. The -**ing** ending is very common.

b a **ng**   h a **ng**   s a **ng**   tw a **ng**

r **ing**   s **ing**   th **ing**

br **ing**   st **ing**   spr **ing**

pi **ng**-po **ng**   si **ng**-so **ng**

l **ong**   l **ong** er

s **ong**   wr **ong**   str **ong**

s **ung**   b **ung**   h **ung**   st **ung**

b **ank**   bl **ank** et   t **ank**

th **ank**   th **ank** you

ink   p **ink**   s **ink**   st **ink**

s **unk**   h **unk**   tr **unk**   m **onk** ey

HU NKY THE PICK UP TR UCK

Hu nk y was a pick up tr uck.

His job was lift**ing** mud and muck.

He sm e lt a bit.

His fr ie nds said, 'Yuk!'

Let's chuck him in the riv er.'

'Help, help!' cried Hu**nk** y,

'I will si**nk**.

Does it mat ter if I sti**nk**?

I'll buy y ou tr act ors all a dri**nk**,

If y ou drag me from the riv er.'

Explain that '?' means a question and is called a question mark.

His sis ter, Hulk, said, 'Let him rot.
Res cue him? No, we will not!
Now I can have his park **ing** sp ot.
Yes, that will be much bet ter.'

Si**ng**, si**ng**, what shall I si**ng**?
The cat has eat en ev er y thi**ng**.

LET THE SOUNDS BEGIN –
A, E, I, O, U

/a-e/ sound (cake, tail)

In this lesson we shall see the /a-e/ sound being spelt, e.g. s**ake** and s**ail**. We have already briefly met the long **a** in the long vowels section on page 51 as d**ay**, m**ay**, p**ay**.

Now we meet other /a-e/ sounds. We see the effect that **e** has at the end of a word. Explain to the child that when **ak** has **e** after it then the sound is long. So that **ak** makes the sound **ak**, but a-k-e sounds **ake**.

Tell the child when sounding out **cake** to say c-a-k leaving out **e** and making the **a** long.

J **ake**	c **ake**	b **ake**
m **ake**	t **ake**	mis **take**
t **ake** n	sh **ake**	sn **ake**

We also meet /ai/. Tell the child that when **i** comes after **a,** the sound is also long. So that p-**a**-d is sounded p**a**d (short **a**) but p-**ai**-d is sounded p**ai**d.

s **ai** l	t **ai** l	pig t**ai** l
w **ai** l	n **ai** l	m **ai** l
sn **ai** l	a fr **ai** d	
g **ale**	t **ale**	p **ale**
wh **ale**		

sp **ade**   m **ade**   bl **ade**

gr **ade**   pr **ay** ed   pl **ay** ed

a pe   gr **ape**

g **ate**   **a** te   l **ate**

pl **ate**   sk **ate**   w **ai** t

str **aigh** t   gr **ea** t   br **ea** k

st **ea** k

r **ai** n   tr **ai** n   st **ai** n

pl **ai** n   l **ane**   pl **ane**

BOOBY TRAP WORD

Straight must also be
rote-learned.

Explain to the child that plane is
short for aeroplane.

/ a - e / s o u n d

s **ame**   n **ame**   g **ame**

c **ame**   fl **ame**

w **ake**   a w **ake**   m **ake**

r **ave**   s **ave**   s **afe**

p **ave** ment

I h **ate** pigs.
I can not s **ay** why.
Is it the smell
As th **ey** go by?

K **ate**, K **ate**,
Do w **ai** t at the g **ate**.
The tr **ai** n will be l **ate**.
I must fin ish this g **ame**.
It's al **way** s the s **a** me.
You nev er w **ai** t.

WHY JAKE WAS LATE

'Late again, Jake?'

'I'm afraid so, Miss Snake.
You see the crazy old train
Made a great big mistake.
It went the wrong way
That's what happened today;
The train went the wrong way,
So that's why I'm late.'

'Oh tell us more, Jake.'

'Well, it jumped off the rails,
Squashed two or three snails,
Crazy old train,
Then straight down the lane
And straight into the lake.
So we all had to wait
Till it came back again,
The crazy old train.
So that's why I'm late.

Remind the child that **I'm** is short for **I am**.

/ a - e / s o u n d

Not my mis**take**.
Don't bl**ame** me, Miss Sn**ake**.
Not my mis**take**.'

'Oh, that's ok**ay**, J**ake**.
We'll stop now for br**eak**.'

Da vid	K ate	A my
Ja mes	A bi gail	J ake
Gr ace	Na th an	Ka ty
Oct a vi a	Mad e leine	
Frey a	El en a	

/ee/ sound (feet, beak)

Here we properly meet the long /ee/ sound. You will find more words with ee and ea that we have already seen in b**ee** and t**ea**. Tell the child that ee sounds /ee/ and so does ea.

Don't try to tackle all these words at once. Choose some lines one day and some another day.

m ee t	n ee d	f ee t	
t ea m	cr ea m	dr ea m	
b ea k	sp ea k	w ee k	ch ee k
ea t	m ea t	s ea t	
cr ee p	sl ee p	d ee p	
f ee l	kn ee l	wh ee l	
m ea l	r ea l		
scr ea m	gr ee n	b ee n	
s ee n	l ea n	qu ee n	
m ea n	cl ea n	b ea ns	
St e ve	sl ee ve	b ee f	
l ea f	pl ea se	t ea se	
ch ee se	fr ee ze	sn ee ze	
p ea s	fl ea s	gr ee dy	

I hate gr**ee**ns.
I can not **ea**t b**ea**ns.
And as for p**ea**s,
They make me sn**ee**ze.

I hate gr**ee**ns
And I hate gra vy.
When I can r**ea**d
I'm go ing in the Na vy.

AT THE ZOO

We saw a snake,
Not yet a wake,
And a sw**ee**t para k**ee**t
Eat a big chunk of m**ea**t.

Fe lix	Ste phen	A me li a
N eil	Pe ter	Gen e vieve
Phoe be	The res a	Se re na
Ka rim	Den ise	Ev e lyn
Em il i a	Ed win a	Jo seph ine
Mar in a	Hel e na	Ev ie

/i-e/ sound (life, night time)

We have already briefly met the long sound of **i** in d**ie**, h**igh** and m**y**. Now we can see more /i-e/ sounds. Explain to the child that **e** at the end of the word makes **i** long so that **b-i-t** is **bit** but b-**ite** is **bite**.

h **ide**	r **ide**	in s **ide**	w **ide**
l **ife**	w **ife**	kn **ife**	
M **ike**	l **ike**	b **ike**	
m **ile**	sm **ile**	st **ile**	
t **ime**	cr **ime**	sl **ime**	
f **ine**	m **ine**		
p **ipe**	sw **ipe**		
s **ize**	pr **ize**		
w **ise**	sur pr **ise**		
k **ite**	b **ite**	qu **ite**	wh **ite**
f **ive**	h **ive**	dr **ive**	a l **ive**
f **ire**	w **ire**	sp **ire**	li **ar**
t **ie**	t **ied**	tr **y**	tr **ied**
fr **y**	fr **ied**	l **ie**	l **ied**

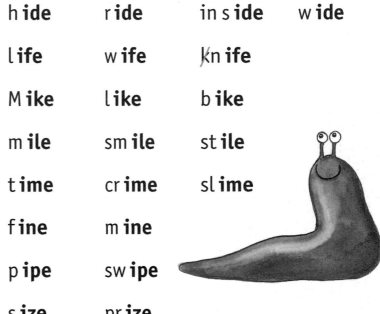

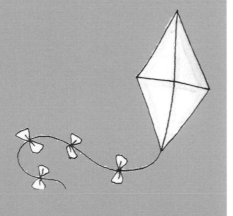

h **igh**   s **igh**   s **igh** t   n **igh** t

l **igh** t   l **igh** t ning

r **igh** t   m **igh** t   br **igh** t

I l **ike** my b **ike**.
I r **ide** for m **ile** s.
And ever y one who sees me
sm **iles**.

In win ter when the fields are wh **ite**,
I sing this song for your de **ligh** t.

One, two, th ree, fou r, f **ive**,
Once I caught a fish al **ive**.
Six, sev en, eight, n **ine**, ten,
Then I let it go a gain.

If you look him
Straight in the **ey e**,
You'll see the li on
Is qu **ite** sh **y**.

BOOBY TRAP WORDS

One is another of these special words that need to be learned by the child. Explain that one sounds like 'wun'.

/ i - e / s o u n d

H i, gu ys.

What a surp r **ise**!

I got a pr **ize**

For the best mud p **ies**.

I clean my teeth

With Teeth o Br **igh** t.

It makes them go qu **ite** wh **ite**.

They sh ine l ike sun l **igh** t in the day,

And l **ike** jel ly beans at n **igh** t.

Soph i a   Mi chael   Mar i a

Si mon   E liz a   Miles

I sla   I saac   Mi lo

Ya hy a   Mi ke

/ i - e / s o u n d

/o-e/ sound (float, home)

We have already seen some /o-e/ sounds, including **bow**, **go**, **Joe** and **no**.

Now we can see some more. Tell the child that **e** at the end of the word makes **o** long so that **d-o-t** is **dot**, but d-**ote** is **dote**.

r **ope**	p **ope**	h **ope**
b **one**	c **one**	a l **one**
l **one** ly	st **one**	ph **one**
c **osy**	cl **ose**	r **ose**
d **oze**	fr **oze**	

n **ose**

Tell the child that when **not** has **e** after it then the /o/ sound is long. So that **n-o-t** is sounded **not**, but n-**ote** is sounded **note**.

h **ome**	d **ome**	
n **ote**	v **ote**	wr **ote**
h **ole**	p **ole**	
j **oke**	c **oke**	sm **oke**
sp **oke**	br **oke** n	

Tell the child that when **a** comes after **o**, the sound of **o** is long so that **c-o-t** is **cot** but c-**oa**-t is **coat**.

c **oa** t	g **oa** t	b **oa** t
thr **oa** t	fl **oa** t	st **oa** t
f **oa** l	g **oa** l	c **oa** l

/ o - e / s o u n d

f **oa** m   r **oa** m   gr **oa** n

m **oa** n   s **oa** p   l **oa** f

t **oa** d   l **oa** d   r **oa** d

s **oa** k

Jan u ar y brings the sn **ow,**
Makes the feet and fing ers gl **ow.**

I like mud.
I like it on my cl **othe** s.
I like it on my fing ers
I like it on my t **oe** s.

Don't forget to take it in turns to read, child and parent alternating with a line each, sharing the reading.

TRIP TO R OME

To by G **oa** t
And So ph ie St **oa** t
Left h **ome**
By b **oa** t
To g **o** to R **ome,**

BOAT TO ROME

/ o - e / s o u n d

98

To see the **P**ope, St Pe**te**r's **D**ome,
and p**ost** a ph**o**to h**ome**.

They wr**ote**
A n**ote**
To th**ose** at h**ome**.
The n**ote**
They wr**ote** was this:
'**D**on't m**oa**n and gr**oa**n,
You f**olk**s at h**ome**,

We'll ph **one**

I h **ope,**

On So ph ie's yel **low** m **o** bile ph **one.**

We'll p **ost** a card from R **ome.**

'We w **on**'t be long

A way from h **ome.**

O n ly a week, I sup p **ose,**

At m **ost,**'

Wr **ote** S **oph** ie St **oa** t.

Explain that **ph** has the **/f/** sound.

So ph ie	Jo se ph	Jo an
Jo el	Ro se	Oph el i a
Jo se phine	Ro sie	Jo an na
Ni cole	An to ni a	Ro man
Zo e	To by	

/ o - e / sound

/**kw**/ sound of qu (quack)

Tell the child that **q** and **u** together make one sound, like **kw**.

ack	**qu** ack
ake	**qu** ake
een	**qu** een
ick	**qu** ick
ite	**qu** ite

Tell the child that **a** here has the /**o**/ sound.

qu ar rel

BOOBY TRAP WORDS

Tell the child how **quiet** and **queue** are sounded. They are booby trap words that will need to be learned.

qu iz	**qu** it	**qu** ite
qu ick ly	**qu** i et	**qu** i et ly
s **qu** eal	s **qu** ash	**qu** eue

Lav en der's bl ue, did dle, did dle,
Lav en der's green.
When I am King, did dle, did dle,
You shall be **Qu** een.

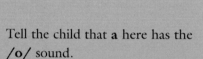

/u-e/ sound (tube, suit)

Again, the letter **e** at the end of a word turns the short vowel **u** into a long sound; so **u-s-e** becomes **use**.

ui is also sounded long: fr**ui**t.

c**ube**	t**ube**	t**une**
d**uke**	f**ume**s	**use**
re f**use**	a m**use**	ex c**use**
n **ew**	n **ew**s pa per	
n **ew** t	f **ew**	st **ew**
d **ew**	f**u** el	
ar g**ue**	res c**ue**	con tin **ue**
bar be c**ue**	fr **ui** t	j **ui** ce
s **ui** t	s **ui** t case	

Ju li a	Ju li et	Juli an
Su san	Su zie	Ru pert
Stu art	Lu cy	Lu cin da
Luke	Bru no	Ru fus

Thom as thr **ew** a mug of
fr **ui** t j **ui** ce
O ver Gran ny's n **ew** bl **ue** s **ui** t.
Tom said he had aimed at
Will i am.
Gran ny said, 'That's no ex c **use**.'

Josh ua   An drew   Hugh

Hu go   Ru by

/S/ sound of c (juice)

We now need briefly to look at the /s/ sound of c as in **nice**, **Lucy** and **juice**.

The time has come to look at **c**,
A ver y use ful let ter.
We know it well in **c**at, **c**ut, ba**ck**.
It can do ev en bet ter.

c can do Lu **c**y,
Ce ci li a, Bru**c**e,
Ni**c**e sli**c**e of i**c**e cream,
And grape fruit jui**c**e.

Lu cy	Al ice	Gr ace
Fran ces	Flor ence	Be a trice
Fran cis	Con stance	Ce ci li a

short /OO/ sound (book)

Tell the child that the **oo** spelling has two sounds. Here **oo** has the short /**oo**/ sound as in b**oo**k.

We will meet the long /oo/ sound as in **moon** later.

Of course, with words such as 'book', 'cook', 'look' and 'hook', some regional dialects give the words a long /**oo**/ sound.

Tell the child that **could'nt, wouldn't** and **shouldn't** are short for **could not, would not** and **should not**.

c **oo** k   l **oo** k   b **oo** k

t **oo** k   g **oo** d   h **oo** d

st **oo** d   w **oo** d   w **oo** d en

g **oo** d-l **oo** k ing

f **oo** t   f **oo** t ball   w **o** man

w **ou̸l̸d**   c **ou̸l̸d**   sh **ou̸l̸d**

w **ou̸l̸d** n't   c **ou̸l̸d** n't   sh **ou̸l̸d** n't

When I was down be side the sea,
A w **oo** d en spade they gave to me
To dig the sand y shore.

The holes were emp ty like a cup.
In ev er y hole the sea came up
Till it c **ou̸l̸d** come no more.

There were two little bears
who lived in a w **oo** d.
One was bad and the other
    was g **oo** d.
G **oo** d bear learned his twice
    times one,
But bad bear left all his
    but tons un done.

short /OO/ sound (pudding)

Here we meet again the short /oo/ sound like book but with another spelling: the **u** spelling as in p**u**t.

p **ud** ding	p **ull**	b **ull**
f **ull**	p **ut**	b **ush**
p **ush**	c **ush** ion	p **uss** y cat
b **utch** er	p **ut**	pain **ful**
grate **ful**	pl ay **ful**	du ti **ful**
beau ti **ful**		

P **uss** y cat, P **uss** y cat,
   where have you been?
I've been to Lon don to vis it
   the Queen.

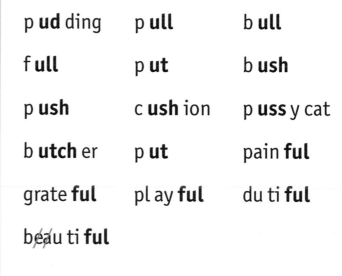

Baa, baa, black sheep
Have you any w **oo** l?
Yes sir, yes sir, three bags f **ull**.

Pease p **ud** ding hot,

Pease p **ud** ding cold,

Pease p **ud** ding in the pot

Nine days old.

Little Jack Hor ner

Sat in the cor ner

Ea ting a Chr ist mas pie.

He p **ut** in a thumb,

And p **ull** ed out a plum

And said: 'What a g **oo** d boy

am I!'

Yu suf   Ed mund   Ab dul

long /OO/ sound (igloo)

Here we meet the second sound for the **oo** spelling, the long /**oo**/ sound as in **moon**.

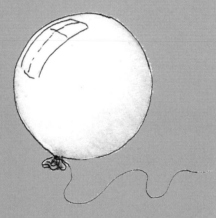

Don't try to tackle all these words at once. Choose some lines one day and some another day.

z **oo**	igl **oo**	sh amp **oo**
f **oo** d	m **oo** d	c **oo** l
p **oo** l	sch **oo** l	pl ay sch **oo** l
f **oo** l	t **oo** l kit	br **oo** m
z **oo** m	ba ll **oo** n	m **oo** n
sp **oo** n	g **oo** se	l **oo** se
r **oo** st	r **oo** f	h **oo** t
b **oo** t	r **oo** t	sm **oo** th
H **oo** v er	sn **oo** ze	ch **oo** se
l **ose**	wh **ose**	s **ou** p
s **u** p er	y **ou** th	do
tw **o**	wh **o**	thr **ough**
can **oe**	y **ou**	sh **oe**

Remember to take turns reading, parent and child.

A kan ga r**oo**

Wh **o**se name was S **ue**

Es caped from the z **oo**

In a bl **ue** can **oe**.

'I'm off to Per **u**,

If I can get thr **ough**

This traf fic qu **eue**,'

Said the kan ga r**oo**.

'Can I come t **oo**

As cab in cr **ew**?'

Said the g **oo** se

Called Br **uce**

Wh **o**'d got l **oo** se.

'Yes, d **o** come t **oo**,'

H **oo** ted the kan ga r**oo**.

'C **oo** l!

Much bet ter than z**oo** sch **oo** l.'

So they fl **ew**

To Per **u**

SOUNDS, SOUNDS AND MORE SOUNDS!

/ar/ sound (bark)

We have already seen what **r** does to **a** in **car**, **far**, etc. Here we see some more **/ar/** sounds as in m**a**rk.

b**ar**k	d**ar**k	m**ar**k
m**ar**ket	p**ar**k	sh**ar**k
arch	m**ar**ch	**ar**t
p**ar**t	p**ar**ty	sm**ar**t
st**ar**t	h**ear**t	b**ar**n
d**ar**n	y**ar**d	h**ar**d
gu**ar**d	h**ar**p	sh**ar**p
arm	a l**ar**m	f**ar**m
f**ar**m er	sn**ar**l	p**ar**t ner
st**ar**ve	c**ar**ve	g**ar**den

Matthew, M**ar**k, Luke and John,
Bless the bed that I lie on.

I beg your p**ar**don,

Mrs M**ar**don,

There's a gir**affe**

In your g**ar**den.

H**ar**k, h**ar**k, the dogs do b**ar**k.

Remind the child that **g** can sound like **j**.

The fr**ie**nd**l**y cow, all red and

white,

I love with all my h**ear**t.

She gives me cr**ea**m with all

her m**igh**t,

To eat with ap**pl**e t**ar**t.

/ a r / s o u n d

Ch **ar** lie   Mc **Art** h y
Hid   up   a   tree.
'Look   as   h **ar** d   as   you   can,
You   c **an**'t   see   me.'

Ed ward	Ch arles	Mar cus
Mar tin	Mark	Z ar a
Al ex and er		

Al ex and ra

Ar thur	Kha lid	Char lie
Fin bar	Tat i a na	Lar a

the two sounds of -ed (missed, patted)

Here we meet words that are spelt as two syllables but sounded as one like **stop-ped** which is sounded as **stopt**.

rub	He rub b**ed** his knee.
crack	She crack **ed** nuts.
lick	The dog lick **ed** my hand.
knock	The vis i tor knock **ed** on the door.
lock	Rich ard lock **ed** his lo ck er.
hug	The bear hug g **ed** the man till he died.
scream	The child ren scr eam **ed** at the snake.

Tell the child to remember to sound all the following past tenses as *one* syllable.

clean	**cleaned**
phone	**phoned**
smile	**smiled**
hope	**hoped**
show	**showed**
brush	**brushed**
share	**shared**

care	**cared**
boil	**boiled**
play	**played**
thank	**thanked**
try	**tried**
watch	**watched**

Explain that words ending in **t** or **d** cannot be sounded as one syllable when ending with **ed**.

pat	Fe lix pat **ted** his dog.
wait	Mar y wait **ed** for the train.
start	It start **ed** to rain.
hate	Ad am hat **ed** thun der.
add	Po ppy add **ed** two and two.
mend	Dad mend **ed** the car.

more /ar/ sounds (nasty, banana)

Tell the child that here we meet more /ar/ sounds without the letter **r**.

All the **a** spellings on this page can just as well be sounded with the /a/ sound and, because of regional dialects, a lot of people pronounce **aunt** and **can't** to rhyme with **pant**.

Tell the child that **shan't** and **can't** are short for **shall not** and **cannot**.

gl **ass**	gr **ass**	p **ass**
l **ast**	p **ast**	f **ast**
f **ast** er	c **ast**	c **ast** le
m **ast**	m **ast** er	n **as** ty
dis **ast** er	gh **ast** ly	
aft er	**aft** er noon	r **aft**
ask	t **ask**	b **ask** et
c **alf**	h **alf**	l **augh**
au nt	c **an'** t	sh **an'** t
ch **ant**	gr **ant**	sl **ant**
c **alm**	p **alm**	br **an** ch
py **ja ma** s	**an** swer	ba **na na**
cl **asp**	r **asp** ber ry	
b **ath**	p **ath**	

Remind the child that **c** can sometimes have the **/s/** sound. It will be properly met later.

f **ath** er   r **ath** er

h **alf**   c **alf**

Fr **an** ce   d **an** ce

A c **alf**

In a sc **arf**

Makes me l **augh.**

As I went out on Sat ur day l **ast**

A great big pig went m **ar** ch ing

     p **ast.**

more /ar/ sounds

There was an old wo man
Tossed up in a b **ask** et
Nine teen times as high as
the moon.
Where she was go ing I could n't
but **ask** it
For in her hand she car ried a
broom.

It's rude
To throw food
At your f **ath** er.
You c **an**'t
Tell your **au** nt
She's a witch.

You're us u al ly hung
If you stick out your tongue.
So be good or you'll end in a
ditch.

M **ar** k fell in to the b **ath** tub
M **ar** k fell in to the sink
M **ar** k fell in to the r **asp** ber ry jam
And came... out... pink.

F **ath** er slipped on a ba **na na** skin
And fell in to the b **ath.**
R **ath** er a gh **ast** ly dis **ast** er,
   I know,
But we couldn't help l **augh.**

Mark	Char les	Al ex and ra
Ar chie	Mar tin	Mar tha
Arth ur	Mar gar et	Mar jor ie
Mar vin	Bar bar a	Mar tin a
Car men	Zar a	Lar a
Tar a	Sar a	

/or/ sound with r (cork, door, warm)

We have already met the /or/ sound in **or** and **for** and **cor**-ner.

f **or** k   p **or** k

sh **or** t   sp **or** t

l **or** d   sw **or** d

c **or** n   c **or** n flakes

n **or** th   h **orse**   c **ourse**

f **orce**   f **our**   y **our**

oar   r **oar**   br **oad**

a br **oad**

d **oor**   p **oor**   fl **oor**

m **ore**   st **ore**   st **or** y

t **or** toise   sn **ore**   e n **or** mous

w **ar**   w **arm**   a w **ard**

re w **ard**   w **ar** d robe   dw **ar** f

w **arn** ing

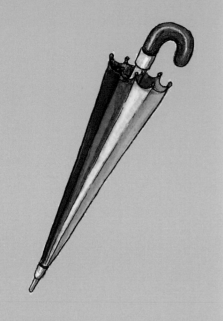

It's rain ing, it's p **our** ing,
The old man is sn **or** ing.
He went to bed
With a cold in his head,
And couldn't get up in the
  m **or** ning.

What shall I c **all**
My dear lit tle d **or** mouse?
His ears are sm **all**
But his tail is e n **or** mous.

LE O NOR A

I'll tell you a st **or** y
Of my friend, Le o **nor** a.
With her h **or** se and her sw **or** d
She trav elled a br **oa** d,
She br **ought** help to the p **oo** r,
And man y things m **ore**,
And killed **all** the mon sters
Who beat at her d **oo** r.

more /ee/ sounds (chief)

Tell the child that the letters **ie**, which you would expect to sound /ie/ as in **lie**, **tie** and **die**, can sound /ee/.

ch **ie** f   re l **ie** f   gr **ie** f

m is ch **ie** f   bel **ie** ve   pr **ie** st

f **ie** ld   sh **ie** ld   p **ie** ce

The ch **ie** f dr **ea** m I dr **ea** m

When I'm a sl **ee** p

Is that I have wings

In ste **a** d of f **ee** t.

It's a re l **ie** f to wake up and

s **ee** my r **ea** l f **ee** t a gain.

more /**or**/ sounds with a (claw, ball)

Explain to the child that all these words with different spellings have the same /**or**/ sound.

Note that the words opposite have no **a**.

dr **aw**	s **aw**	cr **aw** l
h **au** l	l **aw** n	y **aw** n
aw ful	**aw** k ward	
Au gust	**au** tumn	c **augh** t
t **augh** t	n **augh** ty	d **augh** ter
dino s **au** r	w **at** er	be c **au** se
all	b **all**	c **all**
b **ald**	h **alt**	s **alt**
t **alk**	w **alk**	ch **alk**
al so	**al** most	**al** ways
al togeth er	**al** read y	
b **ough** t	th **ough** t	**ough** t
br **ough** t		

G OR DON T OR TOISE AND HIS SKATE B OAR D

'Oh, L **or** d!' said G **or** don
     T **or** toise, sad ly.

'At sp **or** t I **al** ways do so bad ly.

It makes me sick,

I can't run quick.

My fr ie nds are fast,

I'm **al** ways last,

Be c **ause** I cr **aw** l so slow ly.

Then G or don had a wick ed
     th **ough** t.

He went to the shops and there
     he b **ough** t

A skate b **oar** d. 'Now,' he said,
     'I **ough** t

To go so fast

I won't be last.

Now that's a
     brill i ant th **ough** t.'

more /or/ sounds with a

WHY HAVE SWIM MING LES SONS?

Mrs Sn **or** ter

T **augh** t her d **augh** ter

How to swim

So no sharks c **augh** t her.

Her oth er d **augh** ter, n **augh** ty Eve,

Simpl y nev er would be lieve

In w ater sports.

Poor n **augh** ty Eve was w **ar** ned

last Sun day

But a blue shark ate her up on

Mon day.

Hump ty-Dump ty sat on a w **all**;

Hump ty-Dump ty had a great f **all**.

All the King's hor ses and **all** the

King's men

Could not put Hump ty to geth er

a gain.

'Who is that tick ling my back?'
Said the w **all.**
'Me,' said a sm **all** cat er pil lar.
'I'm learn ing to cr **awl.'**

Vic tor ia	Le o n or a	Is a d or a
Hon or	E l ean or a	Cl au dia
Au gust us	Laur a	Ge or ge
Au drey	Gor don	Au brey
Ror y	Greg or y	

more /er/ sounds (fern, work, word)

We have already met some /er/ sounds in **her**, **were** and **fur**. Here we meet some more /er/ sounds with different spellings.

f **er** n	j **er** k	h **er** d
t **ur** n	b **ur** n	b **ur** st
h **ur** t	h **ur** l	c **ur** l
c **ur** ve		

w **or** k	w **or** d	w **or** m
w **or** ld	w **or** se	w **or** th

ear n	l **ear** n	**ear** th
h **ear** d		

d **ir** t	d **ir** ty	sh **ir** t
squ **ir** t	squ **ir** m	f **ir** m
b **ir** d	f **ir** st	g **ir** l
wh **ir** l	st **ir**	

p **ear** l	p **ur** se	n **ur** se
v **er** se	n **er** ve	sw **er** ve

Once I saw a lit tle b **ir** d
Come hop, hop, hopp ing,
And I cried, 'Lit tle b **ir** d,
Will you stop, stop, stop?'

'More jam,' said Ro sie to her
    mum.
'I want more jam,' said she.
But no one h **ear** d the ma gic
    w **or** d.
Mum took a sip of tea.

'Pl ea se pass the jam,'
Rosie said at last.
Now that's the w **or** d to say.
When Mum h **ear** d
The ma gic w **or** d
She passed it right a way.

Twin kle, twin kle lit tle star,
How I won d **er** what you are.
Up a bove the w **or** ld so high,
Like a dia mond in the sky.

Explain that **g** in **magic** sounds like **j** and will be seen later.

more /er/ sounds

Next t **er** m
I'll l **ear** n
To be a w **or** m.

Hard w **or** k,
I've h **ear** d,
To es cape b **ir** ds
Gobb ling you up
If you're a w **or** m.

Hard w **or** k
To keep wri gg ling
In the **ear** th
And not gigg ling.

Her bert	Ru pert	Stu art
Hec tor	Dex ter	Ber tie
Rob ert	Per cy	El ean or

/le/ sound endings (little)

Point out to the child that these are long vowel sounds.

a **ble**   ta **ble**   sta **ble**

cra **dle**   bi **ble**   fee **ble**

bab **ble**   bob **ble**   bub **ble**

peb **ble**   nib **ble**   scrib **ble**

drib **ble**   poss i **ble**   im poss i **ble**

ram **ble**   scram **ble**   jum **ble**

grum **ble**   med **dle**   mid **dle**

rid **dle**   cud **dle**   mud **dle**

pud **dle**

can **dle**   bun **dle**   unc **le**

ket **tle**   lit **tle**   strug **gle**

wh is **tle**   musc **le**

Lit**tle** Pol ly Flin ders
Sat am ong the cin ders,
Warm ing her pret ty lit **tle** toes.
Her moth er came and caught her,
And whip ped her lit **tle** daugh ter
For spoil ing her nice new clothes.

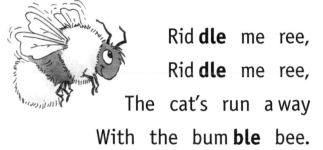

Rid **dle** me ree,
Rid **dle** me ree,
The cat's run a way
With the bum **ble** bee.

Old Moth er Shut **tle**
Lived in a coal scut **tle,**
A long with her dog and her cat.
What they ate I can't tell,
But I know very well
That not one of that par ty was fat.

Jack be nim **ble**,
Jack be quick.
Jack jump o ver the can **dle** stick.

/le/ sound endings

more /le/ sound endings (jungle)

Don't try to tackle all these words at once. Choose some lines one day and some another day.

ap **ple**	dap **ple**	snif **fle**
snuf **fle**	gag **gle**	gig **gle**
wrig **gle**	jin **gle**	jun **gle**
gur **gle**	gar **gle**	par **cel**
cas **tle**	ras **cal**	cack **le**
tack **le**	freck **le**	speck **le**
pick **le**	trick **le**	buck **le**
knuck **le**	tin **kle**	twin **kle**
tram **ple**	sim **ple**	peo **ple**
daz **zle**	driz **zle**	puz **zle**

An ap **ple** a day
Keeps the doc tor aw ay.

The soft 'g' here sounds like 'j' in **gentleman** and **fidget**.

One, two,

Buck **le** my shoe.

Three, four,

Knock on the door.

THE STORY OF FIDG ET Y PHIL IP

Let me see if Phil ip can

Be a lit **tle** gent **le** man.

Let me see if he is a **ble**

To sit still for once at ta **ble**.

But Fidg et y Phil,

Will nev er sit still.

He wrig **gle** s

And gig **gle** s,

And then, I de clare,

Swings back wards and for wards,

And tilts up his chair...

Ab dul   Dan i el

Gab ri elle   Em man u elle

Mi ra belle

/OW/ sound (cow, loud)

Tell the child that **ow** and **ou** generally sound as in **cow** and **loud**.

c **ow**	n **ow**	h **ow**
t **ow** n	d **ow** n	dr **ow** n
br **ow** n	cl **ow** n	fr **ow** n
m **ou** se	h **ou** se	m **ou** th
s **ou** th	**ou** t	l **ou** t
sh **ou** t	a b **ou** t	l **ou** d
a l **ou** d	pr **ou** d	cl **ou** d
cr **ow** d	**ow** l	h **ow** l
gr **ow** l	sc **ow** l	t **ow** el

H **ow** n **ow**
Br **ow** n c **ow**?

Rock-a-bye ba by

On the tree top.

When the wind blows

The cra dle will ro ck

When the b **ou** gh br eaks

The cra dle will fall.

D **ow** n will come

Ba by, b **ou** gh, cra dle and all.

This is the h **ou** se that Jack built

This is the cheese

That lay in the h **ou** se that Jack
 built.

This is the rat that ate the ch ee se

That lay in the h **ou** se that Jack
 built.

more /**OW**/ sounds (our, flower)

Here are more /ow/ sounds with different spellings.

fl **ow** er	sh **ow** er	fl **ou** r
h **ou** r	**ou** r	s **ou** r
p **ou** ch	cr **ou** ch	c **ou** nt
c **ou** nt er	f **ou** nt ain	m **ou** nt ain
h **ou** nd	s **ou** nd	f **ou** nd
p **ou** nd	r **ou** nd	gr **ou** nd
a r **ou** nd	dr **ow** ned	pl **ough**
b **ough**	dr **ough** t	

MISS BROWN

Down on the ground
By the silvery fountain,
With flowers all around,
Our Miss Brown found ten
   pounds.

She shouted out loud
To the crowd
All around,
'I'm proud as proud.
Look, I've found ten pounds.
Now come round to **our** house
And we'll all go to town.'

mixture of /o-e/ and /ow/ sounds
(yellow, cloud)

Tell the child that these words have the /ow/ sound as in **cow**.

Tell the child that **ow** can sometimes be sounded like /o-e/. Explain to the child that these words have the /o-e/ sound as in **bowl** and that the **w** is unsounded.

b **ow**	h **ow**	n **ow**
c **ow**	b **ough**	pl **ough**
dr **ow** n	br **ow** n	cl **ou** d
h **ow** l	gr **ow** l	f **ou** nd
b **ow** l	s **ou** l	win d**ow**
pil **low**	bel **low**	yel **low**
hol **low**	**ow** n	**ow** ner
fl **ow** n	s **ow**	b **ow**
m **ow**	k̸n **ow**	thr **ow**
t **ow**	cr **ow**	sn **ow**
l **ow**	l **ow** er	l **ow** est
thr **ow** n	k̸n **ow** n	

An el e phant trod on my t **oe** nails.
It made all my t **oe** nails go black.
'Do the same thing to him,'
Said my **old** friend, Jim,
'It's the best way to get your
   own back'.

Ap ple y Dap ply, a lit tle
   Br **ow** n m **ou** se,
Goes to the cup board
In some bod y's h **ou** se.
In some bod y's cup board
There's ev er y thing nice,
Cake, cheese, jam, bis cuits,
   All charm ing for mice.

mixture of /o-e/ and /ow/ sounds

more /o-e/ sounds (toast, gold)

Tell the child that here **o** is sounded long as in **roll**, not short as in **doll**.

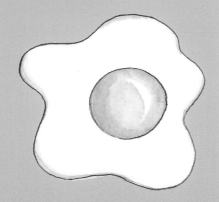

r **o** ll	s **ou** l	wh **ole**
y **o** lk	f **o** lk	**oa** k
o ld	s **o** ld	c **o** ld
g **o** ld	t **o** ld	**o** ld er
c **o** ld er	sh **ou** ld er	s **o** l di er
d **o** n't	w **o** n't	c **o** mb
b **o** th	**ow** n	gr **ow** n
fl **ow** n	sh **ow** n	**o** nly
r **oa** st	t **oa** st	m **o** st
al m **o** st	p **o** st	p **o** st c **o** de

142

Tell the child that soldier is sounded with the /j/ sound.

Oh s **ol** di er, s **ol** di er,
W **o** n't you mar ry me,
With your musk et,
fife and drum?

All that glitt ers is not g **o** ld.
Oft en have you heard this t **o** ld.
Man y a man his life has s **o** ld
But my out side to be h **o** ld.

more /o-e/ sounds

/oy/ sound (noisy, toys)

Tell the child that **oi** and **oy** make the /oy/ sound.

b **oy**	t **oy**	j **oy**
oi l	b **oi** l	b **oi** led
c **oi** l	sp **oi** l	a v **oi** d
j **oi** n	j **oi** nt	**oi** nt ment
p **oi** nt	p **oi** nt ed	n **oi** se
p **oi** son	t **oi** let	an n **oy**
an n **oy** ing	en j **oy**	s **oy** a
oy ster		

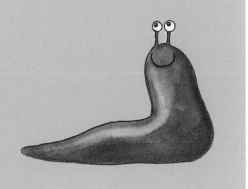

BOYS

What are lit tle b **oy** s made of?
What are lit tle b **oy** s made of?
Slugs and snails and pup py
   dogs' tails,
That's what lit tle b **oy** s are
   made of.

The moon was shining sulkily
Because she thought the sun
Had no business to be there
After the day was done.
'It's very rude of him,' she said,
'To come and sp**oi**l the fun.'

R oy   J oy

more /i-e/ sounds (child, kind)

We have seen some /i-e/ sounds already in **my** and **die** and **high**. We have also seen **like**, **bike**, **night** and **right**.

Here are a few more /i-e/ sounds.

eye   ch **ild**   m **ild**   w **ild**

l **ine**   s **ign**   s **ign**-post

t **iny**   sh **iny**   sl **im**y

BOOBY TRAP WORD

Eye is another one of these special words. With regular repetition your child will become familiar with it.

cl **imb**   be h **ind**   b **ind**

bl **ind**   f **ind**   m **ind**

r **ind**   re m **ind**   gr **ind**

Remember the other **wind** that blows in a storm.

k **ind**   un k **ind**   w **ind**

bl **ind** ness   k **ind** ness   p **int**

H **ei** nz   **ei** ther   n **ei** ther

d **ie** t   qu **ie** t   h **ei** ght

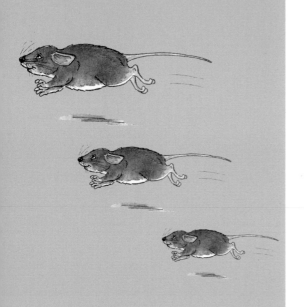

Three bl**ind** m**ice**,
Three bl**ind** m**ice**.
See how they run,
See how they run.
They all ran aft er the far mer's
    w**ife**
Who cut off their tails with a
    car ving kn**ife**
Did you ev er see such a thing
    in your l**ife**
As three bl**ind** m**ice**?

Be **hind** the bl**inds** I sit and watch
The peø ple pass ing – pass ing b**y**;
And not a sin gle one can see
M**y** t**in**y watch ing **eye**.

more /i-e/ sounds

All day long
The sun shines br**igh**t.
The moon and stars
Come out b**y** n**igh**t.

From tw**i**l**igh**t t**ime**
They l**ine** the sk**ies**,
And watch the world
With qu**i**et **eyes**.

I don't m**ind** sp**i**ders.
And I don't m**ind** snakes.
But there's one thing
I do not like...
Aunt Drag on's toe nail cakes.

more /i-e/ sounds

/air/ sound (air, dare, bear)

Here we meet the /air/ sound
as in **airy-fairy bears** and other
spellings.

air	**air** port	ch **air**
f **air**	st **air**	h **air**
p **air**	f **air** y	

c **are**	c **are** ful	d **are**
d **ar** ing	sh **are**	sh **ar** ing
sp **are**	st **are**	M **ar** y

b **ear**	p **ear**	th **ere**
wh **ere**	no wh **ere**	ev er y wh **ere**
th **eir**		

Izz y Wh izz y was a b **ear.**
Izz y Wh izz y had no h **air.**
Izz y Wh izz y was n't fuzz y, was he?

Old Moth er Hub bard
Went to the cup board
To fetch her poor dog a bone.
But when she got th **ere**,
The cup board was b **are**,
And so the poor dog had none.

IS A BEL

Is a bel met an e nor mous b **ear.**
Is a bel, Is a bel didn't c **are.**
The b **ear** was hung ry,
The b **ear** was rav en ous.
The b **ear**'s big mouth was cr u el
   and cav ern ous.
Is a bel, Is a bel didn't wor ry.
Is a bel didn't scream or scur ry.
She washed her hands.
She str aight ened her h **air** up.
Then Is a bel qui et ly ate the
   b **ear** up.

/air/ sound

AT THE ZOO

We saw a h**are**,
And a b**ear** in his l**air**,
And a seal have a meal
On a high backed ch**air**.

I saw a mouse.
Wh**ere**?
Th**ere** on the st**air**.
Wh**ere** on the st**air**?
Right th**ere**.
A lit tle mouse with clogs on.
Well, I de cl**are**!
Go ing clip, clip pet y, clop on
the st**air**.
Oh, y**eah**!

Cl are   S ar ah   M ar y
Cl ar is sa   Cl aire

/**ear**/ sound (hear)

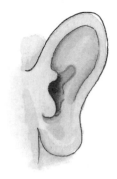

Tell the child that the difference between the /**air**/ sound and the /**ear**/ sound is often very small and difficult to hear. But if he listens to the difference between **tears** from crying and **tears** in his clothes he will perhaps understand better.

ear	**ear** ring	h **ear**
h **ere**	d **ear**	cl **ear**
sm **ear**	sp **ear**	n **ear**
d **eer**	st **eer**	f **ear**
r **ear**	b **eer**	in ter **fere**
app **ear**	dis app **ear**	b **ear** d
y **ear**	t **ear**	f **ier** ce
w **eir** d		

There was an old man with a
   b **ear** d,
Who said, 'It is just as I f **ear** ed.
Two owls and a hen,
Four larks and a wren
Have all made th **eir** nests in
   my b **ear** d.'

Three lit tle kit tens
They lost their mit tens
And they be gan to cry.
   'Oh moth er d **ear**,
   See h **ere**, see h **ere**,
Our mit tens we have lost.'

I said it ver y loud and cl **ear**.
I went and shout ed in his **ear**.

P iers

/**ure**/ sound (pure)

Meet the word **sure** where **s** sounds like **sh** and **sure** sounds like **more**.

c **ure**   p **ure**   s **ure**

y **our**   pict **ure**   crea t **ure**

na t **ure**   mix t **ure**   ad ven t **ure**

cur i ous   **fur** i ous

NATURE STUDY

Mum's such a fun ny mix t**ure**!
She said 'Go and stud y na t **ure**.'
So I plan a big ad ven t **ure**
To our pond to stud y frogs,
And of course I took the dogs.

The next thing is Mum's fur i ous
Yelling 'Kitchen floor needs
   mop ping'
Well, we'd come back wet and
   sop ping
Isn't na t **ure** study **cur** i ous?

/**ire**/ sound (fire)

f **ire**	h **ire**	w **ire**
d **ire**	sh **ire**	bon f **ire**
ad m **ire**	s **ir** e n	**ir** on
pi **r** ate	h **igh** er	fl **y** er
tr **i** e r	dr **i** e r	li **ar**

La dy bird, la dy bird,
Fly a way home.
Your house is on f **ire**,
Your chil dren all gone.
Save for one and her name is Ann,
And she crept un der the fry ing pan.

Frost

Earth stood hard as **ir** on
Wa ter like a stone.

more /u/ sounds (lovely, trouble)

We have already seen /u/ as in **mud** and **muck**. Now we look at other sounds of /u/ as in an**oth**er w**o**rry.

Tell the child that **ou** can sound like /u/. Sometimes the **o** is unsounded.

b **ub** ble	d **ou** ble	tr **ou** ble
c **ou** sin	c **ou** n try	c **ou** ple
y **ou** ng	e n **ou** gh	t **ou** gh
t **ou** ch		

Explain to the child that **o** can also sound like /u/.

l **ove**	gl **ove**	a b **ove**
sh **ove**	**ove** n	l **ove** ly
s **on**	t **on**	fr **ont**
w **on**	w **on** der	**one**
d **one**	m **on** ey	m **on** key
h **on** ey	L **on** d **on**	M **on** day
t **on** gue	a m **on** g	c **ome**
s **ome**	s **ome one**	

BOOBY TRAP WORD

Tongue is another difficult word for your child to learn.

s **ome** thing   s **ome** where

s **ome** times   c **om** fort ab le

un **com** fort ab le   m **oth** er

br **oth** er   **oth** er   sm **oth** er

an **oth** er   **noth** ing   d **oes**

does n't   d **oz en**   w **or ry**

c **ol** our   bl **oo** d   fl **oo** d

Di nah was a di no saur.

Her skin went d **ull** and d **ul** ler.

Her m **oth** er said, 'If you eat
greens,

You'll go a green er c **ol** our.'

Ben ja min B **un** ny
Eats n **oth** ing but h **on** ey.
That's what he eats.
He d **oes** n't like sweets.

D **ou** ble d **ou** ble,
Toil and tr **ou** ble,
Fire burn and caul dron b **ub** ble.

Is that th **un** der
I w **on** der,
That r **um** bling in the clouds?
Or is it for ty e l e phants
R **ush** ing round in crowds?

Did dle did dle d **um** pling,
My s **on** John,
Went to bed with his tr ou sers on.
One shoe off and **one** shoe on,
Did dle did dle dum pling, my s **on**
John.

more / u / sounds

Said Lizz ie,
'I'm bus y
I'm build ing a house.'
'No h **ur** ry.
Don't w **or** ry.'
Said lit tle Miss Mouse.

A mel i a mixed the must ard.
She mixed it good and thick.
She mixed it in the cust ard
And made her m **oth** er sick.

more /e/ sounds (head)

Tell the child that **ea**, as well as having the /ee/ sound as in **seat** and the /a-e/ sound as in **great**, can also have the /e/ sound as in **head**.

This is another example of the same spelling, **ea**, having different sounds: b**ea**k, br**ea**d and br**ea**k. Sometimes the **a** is unsounded.

b**e**d	br**ea**d	d**ea**d
h**ea**d	a h**ea**d	s**ai**d
in st**ea**d	r**ea**dy	al r**ea**dy
spr**ea**d	tr**ea**d	

J**e**ff	d**ea**f	d**ea**lt
j**ea**lous	m**ea**nt	l**ea**pt
br**ea**st	pl**ea**sant	sw**ea**t
br**ea**th	d**ea**th	w**ea**ther
l**ea**ther	f**ea**ther	h**ea**vy
h**ea**ven	h**ea**lthy	

Here is another zany spelling of the /e/ sound. Tell the child that **many** sounds like penny.

m **an** y   **an** y   **an** y thing

any one   **any** body   **any** way

any where

Six and sev en
Go to h **ea** v en.

Come, let's to b **e** d
Said Sleep y h **ea** d.
Tarr y a while, s **ai** d Slow.
Put on the pan,
S **ai** d Greed y Ann,
We'll sup be fore we go.

Spr **ea** d your br **ea** d with d **ea** d
   sl ugs;
Spr **ea** d your br **ea** d with dust.
Spr **ea** d your br **ea** d with rats
   and mice;
Then eat it if you must.

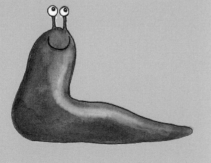

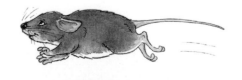

Nich o las N **e** d

He lost his h **ea** d

And put a tur nip on in st **ea** d.

Any thing you can do

I can do bet ter.

I can do **any** thing

Bet ter than you.

No, you can't.

Yes, I can.

No, you can't.

Yes, I can. Yes, I can.

Yes, I can. Yes, I can.

Fi, fie, fo, fum,

I smell the blood of an

En glish man.

If he's a live or if he's d **ea** d,

I'll grind his bones to make my

br **ea** d.

Cats sleep

Any where.

Any ta ble,

Any chair.

O pen draw er,

Emp ty shoe,

Any bod y's lap will do.

Fitt ed in a card board box,

In the cup board,

On your socks,

Any where,

They don't care.

Cats sleep

Any where.

On your marks!
Get set!
R **ea** dy,
St **ea** dy,
GO!

Em il y	Ed ward	El la
Ed mund	El ea nor	Fred die
Ben ja min	Em ma	Hen ry
Hen ri et ta	Hel en	Ben e dict
Is a belle	Al ex and er	Ar ab el la
Geof frey	Hec tor	

/S/ sound of c (face)

Tell the child that **c** before **e**, **i** or **y** sounds like **s**.

c ase   fa **ce**   pla **ce**

ra **ce**   spa **ce**   dis gra **ce**

pea **ce**   flee **ce**   pie **ce**

nie **ce**   po li **ce**   po li **ce** man

i **ce**   i **cy**   ni **ce**

mi **ce**   sl i **ce**   tw i **ce**

voi **ce**   choi **ce**   da **nce**

ch **ance**   Fr **ance**   pen **ce**

fen **ce**   si len **ce**   min **ce**

prin **ce**   prin **ce** ss   on **ce**

boun **ce**   Lu **cy**   jui **cy**

off i **ce**   off i **cer**

ce re al   **cei** ling   **ce** ll

cer tain   **ce** ntre   **ce** nt ral

ce ment   **ci** ne ma   **Ci** n der el la

ci ty   **cir** cle   **cir** cus

cy cle   **cy** mbal   re **cei** ve

ex **ce** pt   ex **ci** te   ex er **ci** se

par **ce** l   sau **ce**   sau **cer**

sc ene   **sci** en **ce**   **sci** ss ors

sc ent

Note that **sc** sounds as /s/ before **e** and **i**.

In **cy**, win **cy** spi der
Climbed up the spout.
Down came the rain
And washed poor spi der out.

Out came the sun shine
And dried up the rain.
In **cy** Win **cy** spi der
Climbed back a gain.

On **ce** I saw a lit tle tai lor
Sit ting, stitch stitch stitch ing,
Cross legg ed on the floor
Of his kitch kitch kitch en.

His thumbs and his fing ers
Were so nim nim nim ble,
With his nee dle and his **sci** ss ors
And his thim thim thim ble.

I think m **ice**
Are ra ther n **ice.**
Their tails are long,
Their fa **ce** s small.
They run a bout
The house at night.
They nib ble things
They should n't touch
And no one seems
To like them much.
But I think mi **ce**
Are ni **ce.**

Lu cy   Ce cil i a   Fran cis

Gr ace   Al ice   Fran ces

Nan cy   Lu ci a   Vin cent

/ s / sound of c

more /**er**/ sounds (learning, work)

Here are some more odd spellings making the sound /e/.

Explain to the child that **ear** can sometimes sound like /er/.

s **ear** ch   h **ear** d   **ear** ly

p **ear** l   **ear** n   l **ear** n

ear th   **ear** th quake

And sometimes **or** can sound like /er/.

w **or** m   w **or** d   w **or** k   w **or** se

B ER NIE THE EAR TH W OR M

B er nie was an **ear** th w **or** m.

He w **or** ked in the **ear** th;

He squ **ir** med in the d **ir** t,

For all he was w **or** th.

Al ways t **ur** ning and ch **ur** ning

And st **ir** ring the **ear** th.

'W **or** st job in the w **or** ld,'

Said B **er** nie one day.

'It's a w **or** m's life I'm lead ing,

All w**or**k and no play.
My sh**ir**t's al ways d**ir**ty, my
F**ur**'s go ing grey.
D**ir**t, d**ir**t, d**ir**t.

'It's my t**ur**n to see life,' said
B**er**nie the W**or**m,
'Chief W**or**m won't like it but
I'm stand ing f**ir**m.
I'm off to the real w**or**ld.
I'll nev**er** re t**ur**n.'

So up in to the real w**or**ld went
B**er**nie the W**or**m.
He squ**ir**med and squ**ir**med
Up in to the real w**or**ld.

But CRACK! WHAM! BANG! DIS AS TER!
F **ir** st there was one big black b **ir** d
Then a sec ond b **ir** d,
Then a th **ir** d b **ir** d with a sharp
   yel low beak.
They w **ere** all look ing for a
   w **or** m for din ner.
'Help!' said B **er** nie. 'Help.
I nev er h **ear** d of this.

'No one said a w **or** d a bout hor rid
   b **ir** ds in the real w **or** ld.
That sharp beak could h **ur** t a
   w **or** m.
What a c **ur** se!
And things could get w **or** se,
   much w **or** se.
I think I pre f **er** red it under the
   ear th.
I'd bet ter re t **ur** n. Too dle pip.'

/j/ sound of g (magic)

The time has come to look at **g**,
An oth er trick y let ter.
We know it well in **g**et and **g**ive,
In pi**g**s and fro**g**s and fin **g**er tips.
It now wants more and bet ter.

Like Dod**g** y **G**eor **ge** and
Gor **ge**ous **Gi**l lie
Who char **ge** and bar **ge**
And man **age** to be sil ly.

Like lar **ge** Mrs Spon **ge**
In her ca **ge** in the dun **ge** on.
And Bri **dge** t the Fi **dge** t
Who drives the fire en **gi** ne.

She plun **ge** d off the e **dge**
Of a le **dge** in the vill **age**
And gor **ge** d at the gar **age**
On saus **age** and cabb **age.**

Tell the child that **g** before **e**, **i** and **y** can sound like /**j**/ as in **gi**raffe.

gen tle	**ge**n tle man	**ge** ni us
gi ant	**gi**ng er	**gir** affe
gyp sy	**gy**m	a **ge**
p **age**	c **age**	r **age**
st **age**	a **ge**nt	dam **age**
man **age**	sav **age**	gar **age**
saus **age**	cab b**age**	mes s**age**
cot t**age**	hu **ge**	a n**gel**
cha **nge**	ra **nge**	da **nge** r
stra **nge** r	or a**nge**	tan **ger** ine
en **gi** ne	fire en **gi** ne	frin **ge**
sin **ge**	dun **ge**on	plun**ge**
spon **ge**	ma**g ic**	ba**dge**

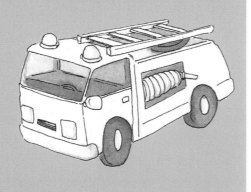

e**dge**	le**dge**	he**dge**
sle**dge**	bri**dge**	f**idg**et
p**ige**on	mar ri**age**	car ri**age**
do**dge**	lo**dge**	bu**dge**
ju**dge**	sol **dier**	lar **ge**
char **ge**	mer **ge**	ver **ge**
for **ge**	gor **ge**	ur **ge**
sur **ge**		

A rob in red breast in a ca **ge**,
Puts all hea ven in a ra **ge**.

Oh, sol **dier**, sol **dier** won't you
   marry me,
With your hel met, belt and drum?
Oh no, sweet maid, I can not
   mar ry you,
For I have no boots to put on.

La dies and **ge**n tle men,
Cats and dogs,
If you eat up your cab b**age**
You'll turn in to frogs.

Ge or **ge** is a **ge** ni us,
And I'll tell you why.
He makes ma **g** ic g a**dg** e ts
That actu al ly fly.

IS A BEL A GAIN

Is a bel met a hid e ous **gi** ant,

Is a bel con tin ued self re li ant.

The **gi** ant was hair y, the **gi** ant
was hor rid,

He had one eye in the mid dle
of his fore head.

'Good morn ing Is a bel,' the
gi ant said.

'I'll grind your bones to make
my bread.'

Is a bel, Is a bel did n't wor ry.

Is a bel did n't scream or scur ry.

She nib bled the bis cuit she
al ways fed off,

And when it was gone, she cut
his head off.

J ohn   Gen e vieve   Ju l i et

Ge or gi na   Josh u a   Ge orge

Imo ge n   Ja mes   Ju li a

J ack   Hu go   Ben ja min

J ake   Jean   Greg or y

Ga bri el   Gi o van ni   Rog er

Another thing to notice about the letter **g** is that **u** sometimes follows it and is not sounded.

gu ard   **gu** ide   **gu** est

gu ess   **gu** ilt y   **gu** i tar

gu in ea pig   lea **gue**   pla **gue**

ro **gue**

/**sh**/ sound (sugar)

Tell the child that **s** can sound like **sh**.

s u gar   **s** ure   **s** ure ly

GIRLS

What are lit tle girls made of?

What are lit tle girls made of?

Su gar and spice

And all things nice,

That's what lit tle girls are

made of.

Some one came knocking

At my wee small door.

Some one came knocking,

I'm s**ure**, s**ure**, s**ure**.

Explain that **s** has a slightly different /**sh**/ sound in:

trea **sure**   mea **sure**   plea **sure**

lei **sure**

Tell the child that the ending
-**tion** is sounded as if spelt -**shun.**

sta **tion**   re la **tion**   no **tion**

po **tion**   con di **tion**   ex ped i **tion**

at ten **tion**   ques **tion**   ac **tion**

fr ac **tion**   di rec **tion**   in sp ec **tion**

coll ec **tion**   pic **ture**   in ter rup **tion**

pa **tien** t   ef fi **cien** t

Tell the child that **sion** and **cian**
at the end of a word are also
generally sounded **shun.**

mis **sion**   per mis **sion**   per cus **sion**

oc ca **sion**   con fu **sion**   col li **sion**

de ci **sion**   ma gi **cian**   sp e **cial**

Explain to the child that **tious,
cious** and **xious** are generally
sounded **shus.**

pre **cious**   de li **cious**   a tro **cious**

fe ro **cious**   scr ump **tious**

an **xious**   ma **ch** ine

wa **sh** ing ma **ch** ine

su per ca li fra gi lis tic ex pi a li do **cious**

/ s h / s o u n d

RE LA TIONS

The trou ble with re la **tions**
Is their bor ing con ver sa **tions,**
Al ways ask ing sil ly ques **tions,**
Like can I read and add.

So I say that I like ac **tion**
More than read ing books and
　fr ac **tions,**
And I don't like in ter rup **tions**
Play ing crick et with my dad.

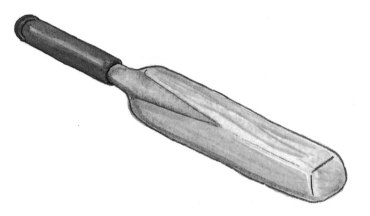

Char lotte　Pat ri ci a　L u c i a
Fran ces ca

/**f**/ sound of ph (phone)

Tell the child that **ph** sounds like **f**.

ph o to   tel e **ph** one   al **ph** a bet

el e **ph** ant   **ph** one

Way down south where tel e **ph** ones grow,

A grass hopp er stepped on an el e **ph** ant's toe.

The el e **ph** ant said, with tears in his eyes,

'Pick on some bod y your own size.'

Ph ill ip   Ph il ip pa   Chr i st o **ph** er

Ste ph an ie   Jo se ph   So ph ie

St e ph en   O ph e li a   Jos e ph ine

Ph oe be

/k/ sound of ch (hi-tech)

Tell the child that **ch**, already met in **chop**, can also sound like **k** in **Chris**.

hi-te **ch**   s **ch** ool   s **ch** ool girl

s **ch** ool boy   **ch** em ist   **Ch** rist mas

ch rist ia n   **ch** oir   lo **ch**

a **ch** e   head a **ch** e

an **ch** or   **ch** ar acter

Ch rist mas is com ing,
The geese are get ting fat.
Please put a pen ny
In the old man's hat.

LO CH NESS MON STER

O **ch**, now I'll give you all a sho **ck**!

In Scot land, in a deep, dark lo **ch**,

There lives a mon ster by a ro **ck.**

It is the LO **CH** NESS MON STER!

My friend, **Ch** lo e, saw it rise

Out of the lo **ch** with her own eyes.

Ch ris to pher says, 'Oh, that's all lies.

I ex pect she saw a lob ster.'

Ch rist oph er	Ch rist ine
Ni ch o las	Ch lo e
Ch rist a bel	Christ ian Zach ary

APPENDIX: THE LAST WORD

PREFIXES AND SUFFIXES

For correct spelling it is important for your child to recognise prefixes and suffixes – they show where a word may be broken up into the syllables essential for decoding it. Take beware for example; it would be easy for a child not familiar with this word to get in difficulties by taking bew together and failing to get the word. If, however, he is aware of the prefix be, that it is a syllable, then he can tell where to break the word up and how to decode it.

On the following pages is a comprehensive list of prefixes and suffixes for you to practise with your child to ensure he recognises and understands the structure of common words, essential to correct spelling.

Prefixes

A

a bout   **a** bove   **a** cross   **a** fraid   **a** gain

a go   **a** head   **a** like   **a** live   **a** long

a loud   **a** mong   **a** nother   **a** part   **a** round

a sleep   **a** wake   **a** way

AL

al most   **al** ways   **al** so   **al** though   **al** to geth er

al ways

ANY

any body   **any** how   **any** more   **any** thing   **any** way

any where

BE

be cause   **be** come   **be** fore   **be** gin   **be** have

be hind   **be** lieve   **be** long   **be** low   **be** neath

be side   **be** tween   **be** ware

DE

de cide   **de** liv er   **de** light   **de** serve

DIF

dif fer ent   **dif** fi cult

DIS

dis ap pear   **dis** ap point   **dis** ast er   **dis** cov er

dis guise   **dis** gust ing   **dis** hon est   **dis** like

dis turb

EX

ex actly   **ex** am   **ex** cel lent   **ex** cept   **ex** ci ting

ex cuse   **ex** er cise   **ex** it   **ex** pect   **ex** pens ive

ex plain   **ex** plode   **ex** plore   **ex** tra   **ex** treme ly

FOR

for ev er   **for** get   **for** give   **for** got ten

for tune   **for** ward

IN

in clude   **in** doors   **in** sect   **in** side   **in** stead

in to   **in** vis i ble

INTER

inter est ing   **inter** fere   **inter** net   **inter** rupt

inter val

NO

no body   **no** where

RE

re ceive   **re** cite   **re** fuse   **re** lax   **re** lief

re li ab le   **re** main   **re** mem ber   **re** peat   **re** ply

re sult   **re** turn   **re** ward

SOME

some body   **some** how   **some** one   **some** times

some thing   **some** where

TO

to day   **to** bog gan   **to** geth er   **to** mor row   **to** night

to wards

UN

un do   **un** dress   **un** fair   **un** hap py   **un** less
un ti dy   **un** til   **un** usu al

UNDER

under ground   **under** line   **under** neath
under stand   **under** water

UP

up on   **up** right   **up** set   **up** side down
up stairs

Suffixes

BODY

any **body**   every **body**   no **body**   some **body**

SIDE

be **side**   in **side**   out **side**   sea **side**

THING

any **thing**   every **thing**   no **thing**   some **thing**

WHERE

some **where**   no **where**   any **where**   every **where**

DIFFERENT SPELLINGS OF SAME VOWEL SOUNDS

The following list will act as a reference guide to help your child with initially baffling words such as 'bead', 'bread' and 'steak', where the same spelling has different sounds; and, conversely, where the same sounds have different spellings as in 'cork', 'course', 'caught', 'nought', 'door' and 'warm'. These words are presented here in groups so that the child can understand that there is a system that works, and that he can use it himself.

/a e/ sound

ay	d**ay**	m**ay**	p**ay**
a e	n**ame**	g**ate**	m**ake**
ai	t**ai**l	r**ai**n	tr**ai**n
ei	r**ei**n	**ei**ght	n**ei**ghbour
ea	br**ea**k	gr**ea**t	st**ea**k

/e/ sound

e	b**e**d	r**e**d	g**e**t
ea	h**ea**d	br**ea**d	r**ea**dy

/ee/ sound

e	m**e**	w**e**	sh**e**
ee	f**ee**l	wh**ee**l	sn**ee**ze
ea	t**ea**m	**ea**t	l**ea**f

/i e/ sound

y	m**y**	cr**y**	sk**y**
ie	t**ie**	d**ie**	l**ie**

i e	ride	bike	time
i	climb	find	child
igh	high	right	night

/o/ sound

| o | hot | dog | pod |
| a | was | want | swan |

/o e/ sound

o	go	no	so
o e	home	rope	nose
oa	soap	goat	road
ow	snow	blow	grow

/u/ sound

u	up	hug	cup	
o	love	come	mother	colour
oo	blood	flood		

/u e/ sound

ue	Sue	blue	due
u e	use	tube	rude
ew	new	few	crew

/oo/ sound

| oo | book | look | foot |
| u | put | push | put |

/oo/ sound

| oo | too | moon | broom | |

/ar/ sound

| a | father | after | half | calm |
| ar | arm | mark | car | |

/or/ sound

or	for	sort	story	north
oor	door	moor	floor	
ore	more	horse	force	
ar	war	warning	warm	
our	your	four	course	
a	all	water	talk	
aw	awful	crawl	yawn	
au	August	caught	because	
ou	bought	thought	ought	

/er/ sound

er	her	were	sister
ir	fir	girl	third
ur	fur	burn	nurse
or	work	word	world
ear	learn	earn	earth

/ow/ sound

| ow | owl | now | town | flower |
| ou | out | our | house | |

/oy/ sound

| oy | boy | toy | joy |

| oi | **oi**l | p**oi**nt | n**oi**se |

/**air**/ sound

air	h**air**	st**air**	p**air**
are	c**are**	st**are**	sh**are**
ear	b**ear**	p**ear**	t**ear**
ere	th**ere**	wh**ere**	

/**ear**/ sound

| ear | n**ear** | cl**ear** | b**ear**d |
| eer | p**eer** | st**eer** | b**eer** |

phon·ics (fŏn'ĭks)

n. (used with a sing. verb)

1 An instructional method for teaching children to read based on the phonetic interpretation of ordinary spelling.

2 Involves teaching children to learn the connections between letter patterns and the sounds they represent.

3 Children begin learning to read using phonics usually around the age of 5 or 6.

To my mother, who taught all her five children
to read, phonically, before we went to school